ARKANA

A History of Yoga

Vivian Worthington, a former Secretary General of the British Wheel of Yoga, has been studying and teaching yoga for over forty years, and has written and lectured widely on the subject. He has spent three years in India, setting up village industries, and now lives in Shropshire, where he is a radionics practitioner.

VIVIAN WORTHINGTON

A HISTORY OF
YOGA

ARKANA

ARKANA

Published by the Penguin Group
27 Wrights Lane, London W8 5TZ, England
Viking Penguin Inc., 40 West 23rd Street, New York, New York 10010, USA
Penguin Books Australia Ltd, Ringwood, Victoria, Australia
Penguin Books Canada Ltd, 2801 John Street, Markham, Ontario, Canada L3R 1B4
Penguin Books (NZ) Ltd, 182–190 Wairau Road, Auckland 10, New Zealand

Penguin Books Ltd, Registered Offices: Harmondsworth, Middlesex, England

First published in 1982
This edition published by Arkana 1989
Copyright © Vivian Worthington 1982

Filmset in 10pt Baskerville by Times Graphics, Singapore

Printed in Great Britain by
Cox & Wyman Ltd, Reading

A CIP catalogue record for this book is available from the British Library

CONTENTS

FOREWORD

A history of yoga for the general reader – clear and readable, without the confusing complexity of the academic tract and yet with its teeth in the facts – has long been needed to serve the yoga public in the West. Vivian Worthington, a yoga teacher of many years standing, writer, and sometime Secretary General of the British Wheel of Yoga, is undoubtedly the man for the job.

No such history has hitherto appeared, as Mr Worthington explains, because of the wrong-headed approach to the subject – which has in turn engendered views even more wrong-headed. This unfortunate circle needs breaking, and this is the way to do it. The book describes the genesis and development of yoga over the centuries as it was shaped and nourished by the great sages and the classical scriptures, and also demolishes a few misconceptions about what yoga is and where it came from. The people, the books, the stream of ideas, and the impersonal currents of history are all there, recreating the living process which brought forth the greatest system of spiritual thought ever attained. This work should provide invaluable service for the growing body of yoga enthusiasts throughout the world.

Brian Netscher
Editor, 'Yoga Today'

PREFACE

Every Saturday afternoon for three years from the age of fifteen it was my habit to go into Manchester to browse round the secondhand bookshops and the reading room of the central library. This was my equivalent of university education, denied to me for financial reasons. During those years I read my way steadily through all the major classics of Western philosophy, and found the exercise thrilling and enthralling. At Gibb's bookshop in Morsley Street the manager tried to get hold of suitable books, and bought back or exchanged for others those I had finished with.

Then one day he handed me a slim volume in faded brown covers, with the remark, 'I think you are ready for this.' It was the Principal Upanishads translated by Max Muller. The effect was stunning. It was so unlike the academic philosophies I had been struggling with over the last few years. The teachings were beautiful and uplifting, but never moralizing, and they went to the heart of the matter as far as understanding the nature of reality was concerned. Western philosophy fell into place as so many word puzzles, mostly trite, through intriguing word games. It seemed that suddenly I had come home. Back went all my other books, and for some time afterwards I avidly read anything and everything on Indian philosophy, and especially on yoga.

For me yoga was indeed a great discovery. Here was a system of thought that also included practice. It included all of the philosophies that Europe had inherited from the Greeks, but went very much further. It also included that other tradition in Europe, the occult, a corpus of teaching and practice that had been compelled to go underground in the dark ages and remain there almost up to the present day. These teachings, so shrouded in mystery and warned against as dangerous, were treated in an open and matter of fact manner that was refreshing to say the least. Yoga also offered a very satisfactory system of what might be called religion, which included the validity of mystical experience, and the practice of meditation. Added to this was a complex and most satisfying system of physical exercises to keep one fit, but also to prepare the body and mind for spiritual enlightenment, perhaps better stated as a vision of reality. Add to the above some very convincing explanations of the processes of birth and death, and the meanings behind these processes, and we have a system of yoga that has dominated my life ever since.

One problem associated with gaining such a mystical opening and vantage point fairly early in life has been a situation often spoken of, particularly by Christian mystics. This has been the difficulty of finding much of relevance in ordinary life that one can identify with or find meaningful. This situation is provided for in India by retirement from the world or taking to the begging bowl. It is not so in Europe at the present time where all are required to earn their living in the prescribed fashion. Only a few farsighted visionaries like Carl Jung have foreseen a situation where mystical experience is commonplace, and society will need to be reorganized to take account of it.

The first meeting with yoga was thrilling indeed, but I did not realize then the further treasures that were in store. True to its name, I have come to realize that yoga really does mean union, the uniting of the higher and the lower, spirit and matter. Throughout its history it has pursued the task of integration. I moved from its beginnings in the Upanishads and Indian classical yoga, largely ascetic and ethical, into deeper layers of the human psyche. First the raja yoga of Patanjali, then the emotional warmth of bhakti, and on into the deep psychological understanding of tantra. I also realized how yoga had formed the inspiration and basis of the religion of Buddhism, and how it had influenced other religions outside India.

Being drawn in to teach yoga in its many aspects, though mostly hatha, during the decade of the seventies I felt the need for a reference work covering the whole history of the movement. To my great surprise nothing existed. This was utterly baffling, but was indeed the case. No history of yoga existed, nor ever had. The reasons why are outlined to some extent in the introduction, but the feeling grew on me over the years that such a book had to be written, and as no one else seemed likely to undertake it that it was I who had to write it.

This is the result. It is by no means the really comprehensive history I was looking for, but a first attempt which may provide a foundation for more comprehensive later works by others. In this hope I offer it to the public.

CHRONOLOGICAL TABLE

2000 –	1000	BC	Indus valley civilization – traces of yoga practice.
1500 –	800		Aryan invasions of India. Vedas and Brahmanas.
872 –	772		Parsva, 23rd Jain saviour. Earliest Upanishads.
700 –	600?		Kapila – founder of Samkhya philosophy.
563 –	483		Gotama the Buddha.
548 –	476		Mahavira – founder of modern Jainism.
	300?		Bhagavad Gita was written by Vyasa. Patanjali's Yoga Sutras.
264 –	227		Emperor Ashoka spreads Buddhism in India and Sri Lanka.
	80		Pali canon of Theravada Buddhism formulated.
	65	AD	Buddhism introduced into China.
200 –	300?		Nagarjuna founder of Mahayana, author of Prajna-paramita
200 –	250		Jaimini – founder of Purva Mimamsa.
	300?		Six Systems of Philosophy.
300 –	400		Asanga and Vasabandu – founders of Tantrism and Yogacara.
	552		Boddhidharma to China – founder of Chan (Zen) Buddhism.
	637		Hsuan Tsang takes Yogacara texts to China.
	646		Sam Bhota takes Yogacara texts to Tibet.
637 –	713		Hui Neng reorganizes Chan (Zen) Buddhism.

686 – 719	Sankara – founder of modern Vedanta.
747	Padma Sambhava takes tantric yoga to Tibet.
1000?	Ramanuja – exponent of bhakti yoga.
1016 – 1100	Naropa teacher of Marpa. Atisha reforms Tibetan Buddhism.
1040 – 1123	Milarepa. Buddhism destroyed in India by Moslems.
1191	Eisai – founder of Rinzai sect in Japan.
1300	Dogen – founder of Soto Zen sect in Japan.
1300 – 1400?	Nath Yogis. Goraknath. Hathayogapradipika.
1357 – 1419	Tson-ka-pa – founder of Gelugpas in Tibet.
1469 – 1538	Guru Nanak – founder of Sikhism. Kabir. Sufi yoga.
1500 – 1600?	Geranda Samita and Siva Samita. Hatha yoga manuals.
1615	Dalai Lama takes over rulership of all Tibet.
1830	Ram Mohan Roy brings yoga and Vedanta to Britain.
1875	Theosophical Society formed in New York.
1836 – 1886	Ramakrishna demonstrates unity of all religions.
1893	Vivekananda brings yoga and Vedanta to USA.
1872 – 1950	Aurobindo – founder of Integral Yoga.
1879 – 1950	Ramana Maharshi teaches Vicara meditation.
1893 – 1952	Yogananda spreads yoga and Vedanta in USA.

INTRODUCTION

Yoga is very ancient, certainly much older than the archaeological record, which is the only reliable one we have at
present. The archaeological finds indicate a well-established
system of yoga practice, which must have existed long before
the figurines and seals that have been found were fashioned.

One of the difficulties of tracing a history of yoga has been
that by its nature it leaves nothing behind except myths and
legends of miraculous powers possessed by some of the more
accomplished practitioners of the art. Only in the last
thousand years or so have efforts been made to provide it with
intellectual content such as would elevate it to the status of
philosophy in its own right. The attempts have not been
successful because yoga is not an intellectual activity. So in
India it has tended to run in harness with the Samkhya
philosophy, of which more later. Yoga has in fact tended all
along to be anti-intellectual, even anti-religious. To be true to
itself it must ever stand close to the spontaneous fount of
human creativity. It is more intuitive than reasonable, more
experimental than formalistic, more other-worldly than of
this world, and more akin to art than to science.

For these reasons it has not been studied in its comprehen-
siveness in its own right, but always as part of other studies. As
far as the West is concerned, where the subject has come up at
all in the universities it has been submerged within the subject
of Indology, or of comparative religion. From the point of
view of the universities, who deal in mental concepts, mind
stuff if you like, there would be very little in yoga to study any-
way. This is to be expected from an activity that is meaningful
only if practised. So until the present time yoga has not been
studied as a subject in its own right in the universities in the
Western world. In fact only about twenty yoga texts have
been rendered into any European language. Some of these
translations date from the end of the nineteenth century, and

make for very dull reading. Most effort has been concentrated on the Yoga Sutras of Patanjali, followed by some of the tantras. The Upanishads have tended to be studied as Vedic, whereas they are yogic. The fact that they were adopted by the Brahminical establishment within Hinduism some time after they were uttered, and later written down, does not mean that their original source was Vedic. The same can be said of many other works as we shall see in the course of our study. The Bhagavad Gita is certainly in this category.

Buddhism is studied as quite a separate subject, as indeed it should because of its importance. But the Buddha is still looked on as a Hindu reformer, and Buddhism as a revolt against Hinduism. In fact the Buddha, though almost certainly brought up as a Hindu, being of the Kshatriya caste, never spoke of trying to reform Hinduism. The teachings he enunciated were of quite a different order and emphasis. When he left his palace and went into the real world he very soon contacted another stream of religious thought and practice, one that was much more naturalistic than the priest-ridden Brahminism that he had left behind.

This stream, which has been called Sramanism (not to be confused with Shamanism) is believed by many to have been the original religion of India before the Aryans imposed their own Vedic religion on their conquered peoples. It is very much older than Vedic Hinduism, and was represented by a great variety of free-thinkers outside of, and opposed to, the Vedic religion of the Brahmins. They were probably equally opposed to the pre-Vedic animistic religions with their emphasis on placating the gods by offering sacrifices, maybe even human sacrifice, and fertility rites of the type that were current throughout the world at that time. The unifying feature of this freelance religious movement was the practice of yoga.

The Buddha came into contact with this movement, becoming as one of them, a wandering mendicant beggar, first absorbing the teachings, trying to find their relevance for him, and eventually putting out his own distinctive contribution. Yoga practice at that time, reduced to its barest essentials, comprised austerity, meditation and non-violence. In his first and most famous utterance, the sermon at

Benares, also called the Sermon of the Turning of the Wheel of the Dharma, the Buddha himself referred to a long line of teachers or rishis who had gone before, and whose line of teaching and practice he was continuing. The full text is as follows:

> To you devout monks gathered here I say that I have seen an old path, an old road, traversed by the supremely enlightened ones that have gone before. Along that road have I already gone. Along it I have fully known old age and death. I have also known the path leading to the end of old age and death. And I have seen Four Truths. These are the truths about suffering.
>
> The first is the truth of suffering. The second is the truth that suffering can be ended. The third is that there is a definite way to end it. The fourth is the way itself; and that is The Noble Eightfold Path.
> And what is that Noble Eightfold Path? It is Right Views, Right Aim, Right Speech, Right Actions, Right Livelihood, Right Endeavour, Right Mindfulness and Right Concentration.
> This Noble Eightfold Path O monks is that selfsame path that has been trod by those great ones who have gone before. Tread you it also.

Although Buddhism has been much modified and intellectualized over the centuries, yoga practice is still central to it. Indeed it has been argued that were it not so then Buddhism would have joined the many discarded faiths that litter the stage of history.

Jainism is another religion that is looked on by scholars as a Hindu reform movement. But again the most cursory knowledge of this unique faith should acquaint the enquirer with the fact that its origins go back well before Vedic Hinduism. Their own teachings speak of twenty-three jinas who were predecessors of Vadhamana Mahavira who is considered to be the founder, and who incidentally was a contemporary of the Buddha. Again Jainism, both ancient and modern, includes yoga practice. In fact no other faith has taken the practice of non-violence to such lengths as the Jains. This extreme behaviour, and a reluctance to marry outside their faith, have prevented it from growing to the extent it deserves to do.

This fixation of modern scholars on Vedic India has so far blinded them to that other stream we have referred to. The Western mind likes to categorize and tidy things up, whereas the Sramanic culture is extremely untidy. It is fragmentary and confused to the scholarly and scientific mind. So hitherto the easy way out has been taken by ignoring it, but really it is all the more reason for studying it. Great riches may be found.

We have already said that yoga has tended to be submerged within the subjects of Indology and comparative religion. It has however received the attention of departments of linguistics. Sanskrit studies are fairly common university courses today, but a knowledge of Sanskrit is not a necessary qualification for understanding the old classics. Some of the worst translations have been made by Sanskrit scholars. The only real qualification is to have practised yoga over a sufficiently long period to understand the teachings not just intellectually but experientially. The difficulties of scholars with Patanjali's Yoga Sutras prove this point very well. The Sutras are merely indications, words strung upon a thread, providing the absolute minimum of grammatical support. Each word is a word of power. It is loaded as good poetry is loaded. Stated another way, it resonates in the mind. They are not meant to be understood, but to be meditated on. So any attempt to present the Sutras as a fully written out text or dissertation is doomed to failure unless the translator has had personal experience of the categories of thought and action being presented.

When the ancient religions of India have been studied under the subject of comparative religion the result has again been most unsatisfactory. Some early attempts by Christian missionaries make very amusing reading today. They were examining Indian religion merely in order to compare it unfavourably with Christianity. This treatment usually involves comparing the lower forms of Hinduism with the higher forms of Christianity. It also often takes the form of questioning the strong mystical element in Hinduism by academics far removed from this experience by their own excess of intellectuality. Even today such books are being written by Christian theologians. Writing from a Christian background, and an academic one at that, such people can get nowhere near the true spirit of the activity they purport to examine.

Yoga requires empathy to be commented on satisfactorily. Scholastic aloofness from the subject, much prized in many fields, is not a proper attitude for its study. Mysticism has suffered the same treatment to the extent that some psychologists have condemned it as a mental disorder, while many theologians have condemned it as an escape from reality. Not having experienced it, nor having the capacity to do so, they do not realize that it puts one in touch with reality in a way no exclusively mental activity can ever do.

So we ask again, why has yoga not been studied as a subject in its own right at our various institutions of higher learning, and why has no history of the subject appeared hitherto? We have already said that yoga is concerned primarily with practice, but the point needs to be further made that this practice is in the main highly subjective. It is not easy to measure or intellectualize. So really the universities, because they deal solely in mental concepts, are not qualified to make such a study. Yoga is therefore forced back into the Sramanic stream, which still runs strongly today under many names, a free-thinking, free-acting, unorganized discipline standing outside of established religion, and outside of any government administrative or educational system.

The explosive growth of yoga we have seen in the last decades has been a spontaneous, popular movement owing nothing to government or official sponsorship or encouragement. This really is how yoga has always been. There was similar popular enthusiasm when it first went to China, Japan and Tibet. Now that yoga has taken root in the West it may be better not to become a subject of study by intellectuals, nor to be state-sponsored in any way. The fact that it has been taken up by ordinary people of all classes, and without any intellectual or religious pretensions, augurs well for the future.

One explanation of why a history of yoga has not appeared hitherto is that it is not yet time: that insufficient material is available. This might be thought correct if one was looking for purely yoga material, and assume that yoga traditionally had been carried on as a distinct activity separate from other religious and cultural activities. In fact this assumption is a great mistake. Yoga has not been carried on that way, except to a minor extent where a guru has gathered together some disciples who support him. Even this has rarely been confined to what we generally understand as yoga activity.

Invariably the guru would encourage his devotees to follow the religion, or join in the general ethos of their immediate environment. Not to do so will render their yoga practice selfish and sterile. In any case the guru-chela relationship is temporary. The disciples drift in and out, and the guru dies. Yoga practice has been handed down from one guru to the next, but this has not been a recognized line of succession as the apostolic successions of bishops in the Christian church, the line of Dalai Lamas in Tibet, or the Khalifas of the Islamic world.

Not only do yogis join in the religious and cultural life around them, but their yoga practice makes them better citizens, and better religionists. The training is such that whatever they do in everyday life is enhanced. The practice helps to knit the social fabric. The practice of non-violence alone has often had a most salutary effect in situations of strain and conflict. The fact that yoga has mostly been practised within the framework of the many religions it has influenced, as well as continuing also outside them, will be apparent as our study proceeds.

In tracing the influence of yoga in the various countries of Asia we shall see how new sects have arisen, how the indigenous religions have become modified, and how yoga has often worked like a leaven causing objectionable features to be dropped or modified. Often disappearing, it invariably re-emerges in another form, or the same form with a new exponent. We shall see how Buddhism particularly has often developed extremely worldly forms, but has invariably returned to its own true path. We shall see how yoga appeared in the Indus valley at Harappa and Mohenjo Daro, perhaps living alongside the official religions of the time. It carried on as Sramanism through the Aryan, Brahminical and Vedic periods. Although fiercely contested and often persecuted by the Brahmins, its main writings, the Upanishads, were later adopted by the Brahminical establishment and tagged on at the end of the Vedas thus changing the whole complexion of Hinduism into its modern form known as Vedanta. Its doctrines of reincarnation and karma were also adopted, and its doctrine of Atman-Brahman as the Godhead replaced the highly confusing pantheon of gods of the Vedic age.

At a time of great spiritual awakening, between 600 and 400 BC two of its greatest exponents formed movements that were to become great religions. These were Jainism and Buddhism. Yoga practice continues as part and parcel of these faiths, as it does of modern Hinduism. Yoga went to China and Japan along with Buddhism but became more distinctive as the Chan in China, and the Zen sects in Japan. Zen is extremely lively today, especially in the USA. In the Moslem world it has worked its leaven through Sufis, and is now doing the same in Christianity. In the scientifically minded Western world it is facing a major challenge, and having its claims scrutinized in the laboratories. Even the materialistic and atheistic cultures of Marxism and Scientific Humanism are taking it up enthusiastically.

The reason why yoga survives, and will continue to live, is that it is the repository of something basic in the human soul and psyche. While more exoteric forms of religion may flourish for a time, along with priesthood, caste, sacrifice, repression, conspicuous wealth, extravagant art, buildings, elaborate theologies or complex ritual, these all eventually expend themselves, and a particular religion either purifies itself or is overtaken by something else. We see this in the rise and decline of the many sects of Hinduism and Buddhism, in China, Japan and Tibet. At such times the yoga stream is turned to with relief, and a new sect will arise embodying many of its features. It has always acted from one point of view as a kind of perennial philosophy.

What are the features that people turn to at such times? They are mysticism, the idea of personal effort and discipline including self-improvement, simplicity and austerity, the idea of meeting yourself and reality through meditation, and the doctrines of reincarnation and karma. In the main yoga invites us to be self-reliant. That we no longer look to exterior forms or to another person to help us. We look to ourselves, and in yoga we find techniques and teachings ready to hand to help us.

Yoga has changed considerably since its early pre-Vedic beginnings. There have been, and still are, differences of emphasis, of doctrine and practice within it. Kapila, an early exponent, was an atheist, as indeed were Buddha and Mahavira some time later. Patanjali, whose Yoga Sutras are enthusiastically accepted by the West, is a theist. So is the author of the Bhagavad Gita, and the later exponent of bhakti yoga, Ramanuja. Some, like Ramanuja, put great emphasis on the guru-chela relationship to the extent that the disciple is actually encouraged to worship the guru as God incarnate.

In the West at the present time the physical benefits of yoga are emphasized. Hatha yoga is so popular, especially among women, that many teachers do not teach other aspects. This is often because they are ignorant of them, and also because the pupils are often not interested. Raja or mental yoga is more popular among men, who usually study and practise alone. This division between physical and mental, which is also to some extent between female and male, is due to the social pressures on men to be active and outgoing and not concerned overmuch with their health, whereas women are expected to be, and undoubtedly are, health conscious.

This pursuit of the physical to the neglect of the spiritual aspects of yoga may be due partly to the fact that no satisfactory modus vivendi has yet been found with Christianity. The yoga doctrines of reincarnation and karma make its spiritual practices unacceptable to most religious leaders, although a sizeable minority of ordinary people seem to accept them. The situation in the West is also complicated by the fact that another ideology is contending for its soul. This is scientific humanism. At the present time yoga seems to be standing against both of these as a third possibility.

Some yoga teachings, particularly the pseudo-scientific ones originating in the hatha yoga era, will have to be modified. Scientific research into all aspects of hatha yoga, including the breathing exercises of pranayama, and mind and emotional control through meditation, is now being vigorously pursued in laboratories throughout the world. Even the reincarnation theory is being researched by means of hypnotic regression into past lives, and into the death experience by accounts given of stages of the death process after resuscitation. From all this is emerging a truly scientific yoga very well adapted to the ethos of the present scientific humanist culture.

Since yoga has never had any formal organization such as the major religions have, this history will be in the form of picking up pieces here and there. In the beginning the influence of yoga can be discerned in the various Eastern religions. Traces survive because the literature of all religions is treated with great respect, and carefully guarded. That literature tends in the main to be a true record, such is the reverence with which the teachings of the founders are held. Other material is found in art and sculpture. Yoga has also left traces in travelogues and anecdotes which have been the subject of popular stories for hundreds of years. Older still is the realm of myth and legend containing material which is often proved to be remarkably exact in the light of modern methods of scientific research.

It is interesting to ask whether anywhere in the world any systems of self improvement similar to yoga have flourished to any considerable extent. The answer appears to be no. There may be many reasons, but the only convincing reason appears to be that only in India could such a discipline emerge, flourish and develop more or less without hindrance. It may have something to do with geography. Landlocked to the north, and with the sea to south, east and west, India had been relatively secure from invasion before the Europeans arrived from the sea, and before them the Aryans who broke through the Hindu Kush mountain range, aided in their superior power by their domestication of the horse.

So in India while the mass of the people have practised the lower forms of religion this other stream has continued, and because it has continued for so long it has had time to perfect its techniques and principles. So in the world at the present time only this system of self-improvement and cosmic understanding holds the stage. Indian syncretism is also a factor: any new teaching or teacher with a significant contribution has always been readily absorbed by the Indian mind, and incorporated into the general religious life. Their doctrine of avatars embodies this idea. This syncretism has always made for stability and peace, but has been most frustrating for would-be indoctrinators of one persuasion or another. Christian missionaries were delighted at first to find Christ so readily accepted in India. Later they discovered that he ranked only as equal to many of the other gods and avatars that make up the religious life of India. A syncretism almost as strong is found in Japan. Even China is the same, except that their own culture is so ancient and stable that change in that country is much slower.

In other cultures where change has been more rapid, often brought about by war and conquest, equivalents of Sramanistic cultures have not survived. In ancient Egypt and Greece there were mystical and magical schools which often had the yoga characteristics of self-effort, discipline, austerity and meditation. Non-violence was not so evident. Some of them also had rather rudimentary theories of reincarnation and karma. They were all persecuted and disappeared. Fragments survived in Europe, disguised as orders of chivalry, of which the Knights Templars were the most influential. Freemasonry also contained features of the mystical and magical schools, but this has now declined into a rich man's club whose members have little knowledge of its early Egyptian beginnings. Efforts are being made to revive the orders and mystery schools of the Western occult tradition, and many of them incorporate yoga teaching and practice.

Now having indicated some of the difficulties of our undertaking we shall attempt to outline a true history of yoga.

CHAPTER 1
Beginnings

The earliest traces of yoga activity were found during archaeological excavations at Mohenjo Daro in the Indus valley by Sir Mortimer Wheeler in 1922. One was a faience seal depicting a man seated in the lotus posture. He is flanked by two human worshippers with raised and folded hands. Behind each worshipper is a half-reared snake. Another seal, in steatite, again shows a man in the lotus pose, but seated on a pedestal. Round him are an elephant, a lion, a buffalo, a rhinoceros and a pair of deer. The figure is four-faced, and wearing a headdress. Another figure is of the upper body only. The eyes are closed in meditation. The cloth on his body is thrown across one shoulder. He is bearded and has long hair. Another figure is simply of a man in the lotus pose in meditation. Similar figures to these were found at Harappa. They have been dated to the third millenium BC.

Other sculptures were found, and evidence of horses, oxen, cats and dogs. There was a remarkable absence of weapons. Both cities stood on the Ravi river, with a distance of 560 kilometres between them. They seem to have been established in mature form, not developed slowly. The layout was extremely formal, with streets running at right angles to each other, with standardized house design. There were some palaces, hostels and workshops, with a citadel overlooking the lower city where the labourers' houses were. There was proof of trade with Sumeria. Flooding appeared to have been a constant problem, and this might have led to their evacuation. However, Harappa may have been conquered by invading Aryans. It shows evidence of fighting and massacre, with mutilated bodies piled in heaps. There is also the possibility of revolt from within, as the layout of both cities point to a very oppressive regime. Both cities appear to have been evacuated suddenly.

These archaeological remains reveal much about the cultural life of North India and what is now known as Pakistan. There was a script, not the same as Sumerian, and not yet deciphered. Trade with Sumeria was made evident, from which one could assume that yoga ideas and practices were also well known across what is now Iran, and as far as the valleys of the Tigris and Euphrates in present-day Iraq. The design of the seals would indicate that the yogis depicted there were obviously held in high regard, and perhaps even worshipped. The presence of horses points to the possibility that the twin cities were themselves Aryan settlements, because the horse was not known in India before the Aryan conquests. The early settlers had probably made their peace with the indigenous peoples but were themselves conquered by a later wave of their own people.

Nothing earlier than these archaeological discoveries has yet been found, but India has always had a strong tradition of yogis, yatis, munis, jinas, and other wandering rishis, seers or forest philosophers. These independent free-thinkers were respected for being outside the framework of the established religion. At the time of the Mohenjo Daro and Harappa the religion of India has generally been described as Brahminism. The Aryan invaders had already established the caste system with the priests, the Brahmins, at the head, followed by the rulers, known as Kshatriyas. The word Aryan means noble. The priests were all-powerful and remained so until the independent free-thinkers gained ascendancy in the Upanishadic age.

This other independent, free-thinking stream in Indian religious life has been referred to as Sramanism. These two existed side by side and were opposed to each other. Brahminism was heavy with ritual, laws and the practice of sacrifice. At the time of the Indus valley civilization, and up to the time of the Emperor Asoka, sacrifice was one of its main activities. Human sacrifice is believed to have been practised during the earlier period, but conclusive evidence has not been found. The yogis and jinas particularly put great emphasis on non-violence and harmlessness to all forms of life so obviously there would be considerable opposition from them to the wholesale slaughter of animals that went on day after day. Most important was the horse sacrifice, in which rituals went on continuously for three weeks. The Aryan religion was brutal and materialistic. The caste system was rigid and oppressive, and the Brahmins wielded great power.

The Sramanas, as the yogis and other independent thinkers and teachers were known, were tolerated when the priests were not strong enough to eliminate them, but were hunted down and killed, or driven out of the area where the priests had full control over the people and the ruler. It appears from early writings, however, that the rulers themselves were often far from happy at the power of the priests, and the Sramanas might have them as powerful allies and supporters. Many of the Upanishads, which we will consider later, were in the form of dialogues between kings and yogis, occasionally with Brahmins joining in. Some of the dialogues also included women, indicating that they were fully emancipated as far as the Sramanas were concerned.

The literature of Brahminism was the Vedas, and this period is therefore also referred to as the Vedic age. There are four Vedas: the Rig-Veda, Sama-Veda, Yajur-Veda, and Atharva-Veda. Each was divided into two sections. These were the samitas and the brahmanas. The samitas were mantras, prayers and psalms dealing with religious ceremonial and ritual. The brahmanas were often analyses and commentaries on the samitas, and might describe their use for particular occasions and rites.

The Brahmins jealously guarded their knowledge contained in the four Vedas. Knowledge is power, as they well knew, so while the knowledge was their monopoly they alone had power over the rest of the community. Today we would deny that any power was inherent in these ancient prayers, hymns and rituals. But these forms and formulas were all part of everyday life, and moulded the whole culture. One had to be a very brave soul indeed to reject it all as so much mumbo-jumbo. Of such stuff were the Sramanas. To avoid persecution they moved away from the main centres of population to settle in the forests, collecting round them in course of time a few students and disciples. For this reason they came to be referred to as rishis, or forest philosophers. Their speculations were to mould history and lay the foundation for metaphysics and abstract thought, and to launch the practice of yoga worldwide.

The Vedas are considered to be the oldest religious books in the world. They are virtually unreadable today, being irrelevant to and meaningless in our time. But Hinduism, or Brahminism as it was known in Vedic times, has always been highly syncretistic. It assimilated the teachings that it once despised and persecuted. So tagged on to the end of the Vedas we have some other writings. These are the Upanishads. Another name for modern Hinduism, or at least for the higher forms of it, is Vedanta. Anta means end. So modern Hinduism is founded on the end of the Vedas; that is on the Upanishads. The coming of Vedanta marked the end of the Vedic period, for after the first Upanishads nothing could ever be the same again. The priests were discredited in the eyes of the rulers and the thinking minority among the other castes, and their rituals and sacrifices were seen to be empty.

The early Upanishads were produced by the yogis and other Sramanas. They will be quoted from at length in the next chapter, but first we will take a further look at the Sramanic stream in general. This stream in Indian tradition was characterized not only by its independence of established religious forms, but also by the practices of austerity, meditation and non-violence. There is no evidence that it was the original pre-Aryan religion of India. Its practices were too austere to have commanded a wide following at that remote time. The religion of the indigenous Dravidian population was probably based on animism and fertility rites. Virtually all religions worldwide had this form at that time.

The last wave of Aryan invaders seems to have arrived about 1500 BC. Thereafter the word Aryan came to have an honorific value. An Aryan was one who was noble, respected and faithful to his religion. They were distinguished from the original inhabitants of the country by their lighter skins. The original Dravidian inhabitants were referred to contemptuously as Dasa. The Buddha used the word Ariya-Sacca meaning noble truth when he preached his first sermon, at Benares.

It is instructive to note that traditional teaching, part legend, part fact, refers to the six ancient rishis namely, Vipassi, Sikhi, Vessabhu, Krackuccanda, Kanakarmuni and Kasyapa. The Buddha referred to them as the supremely enlightened ones who have gone before. The Jain religion which was established in its modern form about 450 BC by Mahavira also claims a long succession of former teachers. In fact it refers to twenty-three jinas before Mahavira. The historicity of one of these, Parsvanatha, has been established beyond doubt as circa 750 BC.

The ancient pre-Vedic religious teachers have been referred to variously as munis, yatis, vratyas, vaikhanasas, jinas, rishis, and even as buddhas. The unifying feature of all of them was the practice of austerity, meditation, non-violence, and yogic breathing and physical exercises. The differences between them appear mostly to have been of belief. Some were atheist, some were agnostic, others were theistic. Some held more strongly than others to the twin doctrines of reincarnation and karma. In the matter of practice the jinas placed greater emphasis on the practice of non-violence. Some, principally the munis, placed great emphasis on teaching subjects other than religion. Some were primarily healers, others were psychics or miracle workers. But as stated earlier the common thread uniting them all was the practice of yoga.

Although most of the Sramanas were wanderers or mendicants, or lived in relative seclusion in the forest, some were settled householders. This was often the case when an enlightened king kept the power of the Brahmins under control. For example, Vajnavalkya of the Brihadaryanayaka Upanishad evidently had many cattle, and was not averse to demanding more from the king in exchange for his teachings.

As yoga has often been bracketed with Samkhya within the schema of the Six Systems of Indian Philosophy, it is instructive to note that the Samkhya philosophy too seems to have had a pre-Vedic origin. The founder of the Samkhya system as understood at the present time was Kapila. He was a teacher of history, and is dated to the ninth century BC. Many legends have been woven around him, and he has become an almost mythical figure. The basic ideas of Samkhya will be considered later.

The abstraction and speculations of the Upanishads were arrived at by the meditational practices of jnana yoga, the yoga of wisdom and knowledge. Several of them mention the vital role that meditation and other yoga practices played in preparing and equipping the rishis for the great intuitive revelations that the Upanishads are. In the Chandogya Upanishad for example occurs the line, 'Is there anything higher than thought? Yes; meditation is higher than thought.' For the first time in history, and by these means, man made the leap into abstract thought. Done once, it could be done again, and philosophic abstraction has now become the accepted methodology in theorizing about ultimate reality. But the Upanishads were the first literary exposition of the method, and their message is alive today.

They were the first yoga writings. Although beautiful they lacked the warmth and comfort found in later classics. As strictly works of jnana yoga they require of the reader some feelings for metaphysics, and perhaps some experience, however slight, of mystical states. Later writings such as the Yoga Sutras and Bhagavad Gita brought yoga down from the abstract level and invested it with emotional warmth and poetry. Later still the tantras and the Hathayogapradipika brought the practices completely down to earth, into the sphere of psychology and human relationships in the case of tantrism, and into the sphere of physical well-being in the case of hatha yoga. But anyone devoted to yoga in all its aspects should tackle jnana, the first of all the yogas.

Each Upanishad was transmitted by a different rishi so there is much repetition. They were written at different times, over a time span of at least one thousand years. So there is also inconsistency. Some of the later ones show evidence of compromise with some aspects of Brahminism. Some of the most recent were actually written by Brahmins. In these it is evident that the main battle has been won, and the message of the earliest Upanishads prevailed. Because of the inconsistencies, and in order to shorten them for our purpose, we present only selections that are unique to each one.

They are usually quite short. The scholar Sankara collected one hundred and eight. Of these he considered sixteen to be authoritative, and to contain the substance of all the others. Ten of them he selected as unique and of lasting value, and wrote lengthy commentaries on them. These ten are known as the Principal Upanishads. In the next chapter we shall look at each of these in turn, starting with the oldest. This can merely introduce the teachings. Various more lengthy translations are listed in the bibliography.

CHAPTER 2
The Principal Upanishads

THE BRIHADARANYAKA UPANISHAD

The Brihad is the oldest and the longest of the ten Principal Upanishads. The title means teachings from the forest. It is in six parts. Apart from some pertinent remarks in the opening verses only parts 2, 3 and 4 are of interest. These consist of dialogues between Gargya and King Ajatasatru, between Vajnavalkya and his wife Maitreyi, and between Vajnavalkya and King Janaka.

'This universe before it was created existed as spirit, as Brahman. When spirit created the universe his inmost spirit entered into all that had been created. It is given to man, rare among created things, to know this. If a man dies without realizing the unity of the Self with Brahman he has not reached the true goal of life. He must return again.'

Gargya came to King Ajatasatru and offered to teach him about Brahman. 'Teach on', said the king. Said Gargya, 'the life of the sun I revere as Brahman'. 'No, no', said the king. 'This is a very limited view.' Gargya tried again. 'The life of the moon I revere as Brahman.' Again the king objected. Gargya continued to offer attributes of Brahman such as the life and power of lightning, space, wind, fire, mirror, echo, shadow, and finally the life and power of intelligence. But they were all rejected by the king as inadequate. Gargya is finally exhausted by his effort and asks the king to teach him.

The king takes him over to a sleeping man. 'Now that this man is asleep', said the king, 'he moves around in dreams. His world is a dream world. Using all his senses he roves around in the world of dreams. But when he goes into deeper sleep he is conscious of nothing at all. He enters deep into his own Self. All the powers of life, and the elements of creation are

contained deep in his own Self, to be drawn on and experienced. The Self is everything, and everything is the Self.

All things exist for the Self. The Self is nearer to us than
anything else. If a man worships Brahman, thinking that
Brahman is one thing or another he does not realize the
truth. Nor can he achieve the bliss of liberation. Even a righteous person cannot enjoy eternal life. The good results of his
good deeds will eventually be exhausted, and he will return
again to earth. Only the virtue of he who meditates on the
Self is inexhaustible, for the Self is the source of all virtue.'

Janaka, King of Videha, invited the wise men of Kuru and
Panchala to a contest. The wisest of them would receive
1,000 cows. The king asked who was the wisest. Vajnavalkya
stepped forward and asked for the cows. Everybody was
shocked by his effrontery, whereupon the king and others
began to question him.

Asked Ushasta, 'What is that Spirit which though unseen is
known, and which lives in the heart of all?'

'Your own Self lives in the hearts of all. You cannot see the
seer of the sight, the hearer of the sound, the thinker of the
thought, the knower of the known. Your own Self lives in the
hearts of all. Nothing else matters.'

Asks Kahola, 'Which self is in the hearts of all?'

'It is that Self which rises above hunger and thirst, grief and
deprivation, decay and death. Having realized that Self the
wise lose all craving. They lose craving not only for things of
this world, but also for things of the next. All desires and
cravings are extinguished.'

Asked Uddalaka, 'Do you know that thread on which this
life, the next life, and all beings are strung together? Do you
know that inner ruler who controls this life, the next life, and
all beings?'

'The subtle principle of life is that thread on which this life,
the next, and all beings are strung together. This subtle
principle is the sustainer of life. The inner ruler is that which
dwells in water, but is separate from water, whom water does
not know, whose body water is, and who controls water from
within. This inner ruler is the Self, the immortal. He dwells in
earth and heaven, sun and moon, smell, speech, sight and

hearing, in the mind and in the intellect. Unseen he is the seer, unheard he is the hearer, unthought he is the thinker, unknown he is the knower. He is the Self, the inner ruler, the immortal.'

Then spoke Gargi, daughter of Vachaknu, 'What is that which is above heaven, below earth, and also between heaven and earth?'

'It is prana, the divine energy that sustains the life of all these things.'

'Well spoken', said Gargi. 'Now another question. Since everything in creation is interwoven with everything else, what of Spirit, which stands above creation. In what is Spirit interwoven?'

'That question takes us beyond the point where thought can reach. Spirit is beyond the mind, and beyond questionings. It is profitless to try to transcend the limit.'

The assembled company fell silent, and Vajnavalkya drove the cows away.

On a later occasion King Janaka sat to give audience to such of his subjects as wished to speak to him. Towards the end of the audience he saw Vajnavalkya there. 'What brings you here?' he said. 'Is it cows or philosophy?'

'Both your majesty. I would like to know what your teachers have recently taught you.'

'Jitwa has taught me that word is Brahman, Barku that sight is Brahman, Gardabivipati that hearing is Brahman, Satyakama that mind is Brahman, Vidaghda that the heart is Brahman.'

'Your majesty has equipped himself well for the journey through life. How will you fare when you leave this body?'

'That I do not know.'

'You have attained to the position of one who is free from fear, and who is free from birth and death. You will fall into dreamless sleep and become identified with the Supreme Self, that which can only be described as Not this-Not that.'

Said King Janaka, 'Explain to me this self.'

'That self-luminous being who dwells in the lotus of the heart, surrounded by the senses and the sense organs, and who is the light of the intellect is that Self. He is the light within; knowledge itself. We alternate between sleeping and waking. In sleep we are dreaming. In waking we are thinking. We have two homes, heaven and earth. But there is also a less substantial one between the two. This is the world of dreams. On our nightly journey back to heaven we make dreams by our own power. We make horses, roads, chariots and all sorts of happiness and misery. There we are the creator. But further along the road of our nightly journey we reject all these images, and sink into dreamless sleep.

The Self, the solitary bird, leaves the nest, the body, in charge of its guardian, which is the energy and spark of life and wanders never weary. The Self goes hither and thither, delighting in food, sex and the laughter of friends. He sees the play of all this. No one sees him. The Self shines by its own light.'

Said Janaka, 'What you say delights me. I give you a thousand cows.'

'The Self awakes, and goes about the business of daily life, and at night-time hurries back to his dreams. Having enjoyed his dreams he again returns to conscious life. But nothing of all this clings to the essential Self. As a large fish moves from one bank of a river to the other, Self moves between waking and sleeping. And as an eagle in the sky finally folds its wings with weariness and drops into its nest, so the Self drops into that deeper sleep where he desires nothing, creates nothing and does not dream.

The true nature of the Self is to be free from fear, free from desire and evil. As lovers in deep embrace forget everything, and only feel peace all round, so man where he embraces his true Self feels peace all round. In that state there is neither father nor mother, there are no gods, no worlds, no good and no evil. He neither sees, hears, tastes, smells, knows nor touches. Yet he can see, for sight and he are one; can hear, for sound and he are one; can taste, for taste and he are one; can smell, for smell and he are one; can know, for knowledge and he are one; can touch, for touch and he are one. The Self is eternal and immortal, the one without a second. The Self is the kingdom of Brahman, man's highest goal and greatest bliss. Most creatures can experience only a small part of this bliss. Man is indeed fortunate.'

King Janaka said, 'Speak on sir, another thousand cows are yours.'

'When a man is about to die the lower Self groans like a heavily laden cart. Then the higher Self takes charge and prepares for the journey. The dying man becomes weak, and apparently unconscious. He gathers his powers and senses together, and unites them with his soul-body. Then by the light of the Self life departs from the body through the eye, or the gate of the skull, or by one of the other apertures of the body. But the Self remains conscious, and conscious the dying man goes on his journey. The deeds of his life, and their results, go with him.

As the caterpillar on reaching the end of a blade of grass takes hold of another blade, and draws his body from the first, so the self having reached the end of this body enters into a new one. Or as a goldsmith in the bazaar takes an old vase, melts it down and beats it into a new one, so the Self after death eventually returns in a new vessel, more perfect, perhaps a human body, or perhaps in the body of one of the celestial beings.

A man acts according to his desires. After death he goes to the next world, bearing the subtle impression of his deeds. He returns with the same desires, and so continues subject to rebirth. But he who has conquered desire need not return. In full realization of the Self he also realizes Brahman, and becomes one with Brahman. The path of liberation from desire is hard and long. Only by treading this path can you realize Brahman. Those who tread this path have no desire for progeny, wealth or power. Evil is burned away. He is freed from evil, desire and doubt. Try to attain this, O King.'

Said Janaka, 'Sir, I offer you the whole empire of Videha and myself as your servant.'

Vajnavalkya, having decided to become a hermit, settled all his possessions on his wife Maitreyi, and on leaving spoke to her these words. 'Believe me my dear it is not the husband that is loved; it is the Self. It is not the wife that is loved; it is the Self. Nor is it children, wealth, status, animals, nor anything at all. Nothing is loved for its own sake. It is only the Self that is loved. If a person thinks that any of these things are other than the Self they will abandon him, for they only have life in the Self.

When music is played the separate notes are not heard apart from the whole tune. Only in the whole are the parts known. The Self is that whole. Only by knowing the Self can all the separate elements be known. When the Self is known individuality is lost. When living in the state of individuality one sees, hears, feels and knows another. But when you have realized that everything is spirit, and that spirit is identical with one's own Self how can one see, hear, feel and know another? By whom shall the knower be known?

THE CHANDOGYA UPANISHAD

This Upanishad contains the story of Svetaketu, the boy who was sent away by his father to be educated. He returned at the age of twenty-four, proud of his learning and having a high opinion of himself. His father seeing this said, 'Svetaketu, you are learned and proud, and have a high opinion of yourself. Have your teachers explained to you that knowledge by which all else is known? That knowledge whereby what is not heard is heard, what is not seen is seen. What is not thought is thought?'

'What is this knowledge father?'

'Just as by knowing a lump of clay all that is clay can be known, since any differences are only words, and the reality is clay. The same with gold, iron or any other element, any differences are only words and the reality is that element. So it is with this knowledge.'

'Tell me more father.'

'Bring me a fruit of the banyan tree. Now break it open. What do you see?'

'Very small seeds.'

'Break one of them open. Now what do you see?'

'Nothing.'

'My son, from the very essence of the seed which you cannot see comes this vast banyan tree. Believe me my son, an

invisible and subtle essence is the spirit of the whole universe.
That is reality. That is Atman. You are it.'

'Tell me more father.'

'Place this lump of salt in this water, and come back
tomorrow morning.'

When Svetaketu returned the following morning his father
said to him, 'give me the lump of salt you put into the water
last night.'

'I cannot father. It is dissolved.'

'Now taste the water.'

'It is salty', said Svetaketu.

Said his father, 'In the same way as salt was dissolved in the
water an invisible and subtle essence pervades the whole
universe. That is spirit. That is reality. That is truth, and you
are it.'

THE KATHA UPANISHAD

The text begins with the story of the boy Natchiketas who is
granted three boons by Yama, the god of death. The first two
concern the boy's family, and are granted immediately, but
Yama demurs at the third, and pleads with Natchiketas to ask
for something else. But the boy insists, and Yama lets him
have his way. So follows the famous dialogue with death
which is the heart of the Upanishad.

Natchiketas asks, 'When a man dies, does he exist, or does
he not exist?'

Death replies, 'I cannot answer your question directly, but
this I will say: there is the path of joy, and there is the path of
pleasure. Both attract the soul. Who follows the first aspires
upwards. Who follows the second makes no progress. The
wise take the path of joy. Fools take the path of pleasure. You,
Natchiketas have taken the path of joy. You have not
accepted that chain of possessions wherewith men bind
themselves, and beneath which they sink.

There is the path of knowledge and the path of ignorance.
They lead to different ends. You, Natchiketas, follow the
path of knowledge. If pleasure comes you enjoy it, but you do
not seek it. What lies beyond life cannot show itself to the

childish, the careless, or those deluded by wealth or power. "This is the only world", they say, "there is no other". So they go round from death to death, in ignorance.

The spiritual life cannot be realized by thought and reason, but it can be demonstrated by a guru who has realized it for himself. Truly great is he who can teach of Brahman. Wise is he who can be taught. Favoured is he who understands. You, Natchiketas, have found the best possible teacher. Would that I had another student like you.'

Natchiketas asks, 'What is there between right and wrong, beyond cause and effect, and beyond time?'

Death replies, 'I will give you the sacred word that expresses all the highest things, and all the highest actions and longings. That word is AUM. It represents Brahman. When it is fully understood the end is reached. It is the supreme means of salvation.

Deep in the heart of man is the Atman. It is never born, and never dies. If the slayer thinks he slays, and the slain thinks that he dies, then neither knows the way of truth. The eternal in man cannot kill. The eternal in man cannot die. The Atman is lord of the chariot. Your body is the chariot. Reason is the charioteer, and the mind the reins. One who has right understanding, and whose mind is steady is a good charioteer with well-trained horses.

Beyond the senses are their objects. Beyond the objects is the mind. Beyond the mind is pure reason, and beyond reason is the spirit of man. Beyond the spirit in man is the spirit in the universe, and beyond that is the spirit supreme. Beyond that is nothing. It is the end of the path. The Lords of Creation made the senses in man to turn outwards to the world of sense objects, not to the spirit within. The foolish follow the objects of sense, and so continue in the round of death and rebirth. But the truly wise look within, and find great riches there. Eternity is there, not the transient.

Who sees the many and not the one wanders on from death to death. This truth cannot be learnt even by the mind. It can only be learnt by the practice of yoga. When the senses and the mind are still, and reason itself rests in silence, then begins the path supreme. This calm steadiness of the senses is called yoga. But in treading this path be watchful, for yoga comes and goes. It is difficult to hold this state for very long at any one time. Radiating from the heart are one hundred and one channels. One of these rises to the thousand-petalled lotus above the head. If at death the vital force passes upward to this channel he achieves immortality. If it leaves by any other channel that person remains subject to death and rebirth. Nurture this narrow way.'

So Natchiketas learnt from death the supreme wisdom, and the way to self-realization by the practice of yoga. He united himself with Brahman the supreme spirit, as can anyone who finds Atman, his own higher Self.

PRASNA UPANISHAD

This is the upanishad of the six questions, asked of the sage Pippilada by his students.

Asks Kabandhi, 'How came creation?'

Says Pippilada, 'Sun is life, moon is matter, prana, the primal energy or life force is present in both life and matter. The interaction of these three produces all manifested things.'

Asks Bhargava, 'What are the most important elements in creation?'

Says Pippilada, 'They are space, air, fire, water, earth, voice, mind, eye and ear. But they are all subservient to prana which contains them all.'

Asks Kausalya, 'How does life enter this body, sustain it and leave it?'

Says Pippilada, 'Life comes from spirit. As we cast a shadow, so the spirit casts the shadow of life, and as a shadow of former lives a new life enters this body. Prana is the power of life, and rules all the other powers of the body. These others are Apana, ruling the lower regions, Samana the middle regions, Atman – the self, dwelling in the heart. In the many little channels rising from the heart moves the power of Vyana. Rising from one of them is the power of Udana. This leads to heaven by pure action, and to hell by evil action, or in the average person having a mixture of both, back to this world. Space is Samana, air is Vyana, fire is Udana, earth is

Apana, the spirit in man is Atman. This is the fivefold division of life in the body. Know this, and know that Prana is the life of the whole universe.'

Asks Gargya, 'How many powers sleep in man, and how many remain awake?'

Says Pippilada, 'When darkness falls the powers of the senses become one in the higher powers of the mind. A person neither sees, hears, smells, tastes nor touches, neither speaks, receives, gives, moves nor loves. He sleeps. But the living powers of the body are awake. In dreams the mind remembers, but when mind is overcome by its own radiance it no longer dreams. Joy and peace come to the body. The spirit of man finds peace in union with the Spirit Supreme.'

Asks Salyakama, 'If a person has meditated on AUM for a whole lifetime what happens to him after death?'

Says Pippilada, 'AUM is the sacred word signifying supreme spirit. It has three sounds A, U, M. One whose meditation can only embrace the first sound is benefited thereby and will return to earth for a further incarnation. One whose meditation can embrace the first two sounds will enjoy the joys of heaven for a time, but still return to earth. But one whose meditation can embrace all three sounds goes to heaven, and returns no more to earth.'

Asks Sukesha, 'What is the spirit of sixteen forms?'

Says Pippilada, 'The spirit of sixteen forms arises in the body. The spirit evolved prana, life, faith, space, air, light, water, earth, senses, mind, food, strength, austerity, sacred writings, world and name. These sixteen forms find rest in the spirit as sixteen spokes find rest in the centre of a wheel.'

SVETASVATARA UPANISHAD

This is named after the rishi Svetasvatara.

When the soul takes the form of a body, by that same body the soul is bound. The soul unfolds into a body with dreams and desires, and the urge to live. Its body and its birth are determined by its former works. The quality of the soul will determine its future body; earthy or airy, heavy or light. Its thoughts and actions can lead it to bondage in life after life.

But when one realizes his unity with Brahman he leaves behind his bodies of transmigration.

This vast universe is a wheel. Revolving on it are all living things; on the eternal round of birth, death, rebirth on and on. It is the Wheel of Brahman. The individual is bound to the wheel until by his own insights and intuitions he can free himself from it. Only Brahman is the substance, all else is shadow – maya. Matter and mind are united by maya. Meditate on these and realize they are only three aspects of Brahman. Only by uniting oneself with the substance will one be free of illusion.

Meditate on pure consciousness. Use mind and intellect to prevent the senses attaching themselves to sense objects. Unite your heart with the infinite. Sit with body held upright, and head and neck in a perfectly straight line. When the body is in perfect steadiness breathe rhythmically with a peaceful ebbing and flowing of breath. Find a quiet retreat for the practice of yoga, solitary, sheltered from wind and rain, level and clean, free from dust, and where sight of water and beautiful scenery will uplift thought and contemplation.

As a soiled piece of metal becomes bright and shining when clean, so the yogi becomes radiant. When he has gained power over his body, composed as it is of the elements of earth, air, water, fire and ether, then he obtains a new body of spiritual fire which is beyond illness, old age and death. First fruits of the practice of yoga are health, energy, little waste matter, a clear complexion, lightness of body, a pleasant scent, a controlled voice, and an absence of greedy desires. Then the soul in the yogi shines forth. He realizes everything is spirit. His life is fulfilled. He is forever after without sorrow.

TAITTIRIYA UPANISHAD

The title is given by the name of the rishi who gave out the teachings. The work quotes from various ancient texts, most of which are now lost. Among them are the following:

What must the student practise?

Righteousness, and sacred study and teaching.
Truthfulness, and sacred study and teaching.
Meditation, and sacred study and teaching.
Austerity, and sacred study and teaching.
Humility, and sacred study and teaching.
Reverence, and sacred study and teaching.
Compassion, and sacred study and teaching.

The core of the Upanishad is the account of Brigu the
student, who tries to realize the nature of Brahman. Brigu
went to his father and said, 'Explain to me the nature of
Brahman.'

Said his father, 'Go away and pray for this knowledge.
Meditate on what are the most important elements in life and
in the whole of creation, and tell me what you discover.'

Brigu went away and prayed for a long time, and decided
that Brahman was food, the sustainer of life. He returned to
his father and told him. His father sent him away again. He
again prayed, and decided that Brahman was life itself. His
father again sent him away. Again he prayed and decided that
Brahman was mind. Again his father sent him away. Again he
prayed and decided that Brahman was reason. Again his
father sent him away.

Finally Brigu went away and prayed for a very long time.
Then suddenly he realized Brahman as joy, and experienced
this joy himself. His father was very happy that his son now
knew the nature of Brahman.

The Upanishad then goes on to describe this joy as
experienced by an ascending order of the angelic hierarchies:

The joy of a youthful enlightened person is minute
    compared to that of the Gandharvas.
The joy of the Gandharvas is minute compared to the joy of
    the Devas.
The joy of the Devas is minute compared to the joy of the
    Karma Pitris.
The joy of the Pitris is minute compared to the joy of the
    Devas.
The joy of the Karma Devas is minute compared to the joy
    of the Rupa Devas.

The joy of the Rupa Devas is minute compared to the joy of Indra.

The joy of Indra is minute compared to the joy of Brihaspati.

The joy of Brihaspati is minute compared to the joy of Prajapati.

The joy of Prajapati is minute compared to that of Brahma – the god of creation.

The human being has several bodies.

First the physical body, sustained by food, which eventually must die.

Second the etheric body, encased in the physical, and having the same form.

Third is the astral body.

Fourth is the mental body.

Fifth is the ego.

Sixth is the Atman.

Seventh is Brahman, with whom we are forever joined.

MUNDAKA UPANISHAD

Mundaka means razor. The razor which cuts the knot of ignorance. This Upanishad speaks first of the higher and lower wisdoms, and later of the higher and lower selves of man. It begins:

Angiras asks of Saunaka, 'Master, what is that which when known all else is known?'

Saunaka replies, 'There are two kinds of wisdom, the higher and the lower. The lower wisdom is the four vedas, and the six kinds of knowledge: science and logic, magic and astrology, art and poetry. Those practising the lower wisdom will work for charity, make sacrifices or become learned. Imagining these as the final goal they do not see a higher path. The unwise who praise them as the highest end go to old age and death again. When they go to heaven their good acts are rewarded, but great is their grief when the enjoyment of their reward comes to an end. They inevitably return to earth.

Only the higher wisdom leads to the eternal. Those who live in purity and faith, live in solitude and long not for the earthly possessions, they only recognize the higher wisdom. They go after death to the place of pure spirit and there dwell in eternity.

Brahman is the target to be aimed at all the time. Take the great bow of the Upanishads, and place in it an arrow sharp with devotion. Draw the bow concentrating on him, and hit the centre of the mark. The bow is the sacred AUM, the arrow is the soul. Brahman is the target. As the arrow becomes one with the target, so the watchful soul becomes one with Brahman. Meditate on AUM, and on the Atman.

There are two birds on a tree. The one on the lower branches is of gorgeous plumage. It eats the fruits of the tree, sings and preens its feathers. Its companion on the higher branches is of sombre plumage, is silent and watches over its companion. The bird on the lower branches is the lower self, absorbed in living and activity. The bird on the higher branches is the higher self, at one with spirit. The lower self while still absorbed in living, must at all times recognize its higher Self which watches over it, and is at one with pure spirit.

Whatsoever the pure in heart desire they will attain. Those who wander mainly among earthly desires come back to earth to gratify them. But those who have found fulfilment, even in this life their earthly desires will fade away. They will realize the Atman, the self. They have found the spirit in all, and will go into the All. In truth those who know Brahman become Brahman.'

THE ISA UPANISHAD

This is the shortest of all the Upanishads. The title is taken from the first word of the text, Isa being one of the names of God. At its core are the verses:

'Who sees the Self in all things and all things in the Self has love for all, and is free of ignorance.
Into deep darkness fall those concerned only with action.
Into deeper darkness fall those concerned only with knowledge.

The enlightened use action and knowledge equally, to
overcome fear of death, and attain to immortality.
Into deep darkness fall those concerned only with the
physical.
Into deeper darkness fall those concerned only with the
spiritual.
The enlightened use both physical and spiritual to overcome fear of death, and attain immortality.'

There is much more in the same vein. It ends with the
reminder that continual striving is necessary to achieve and
maintain integration in ourselves, and understanding of the
meaning and purpose of existence, and ends:

'May the soul go to eternal life, and the body go to ashes,
May the soul remember past strivings as it goes.'

THE MANDUKYA UPANISHAD

The title is taken from the rishi Mandukya. Its main interest is
where at one point it speaks of the four states of consciousness, and invokes the sacred word AUM to help us recognize,
realize and meditate on them. This it does by identifying each
state by a particular sound within the all-embracing mantra
AUM.

'AUM contains three sounds, and consciousness comprises
four states.
The first state is waking life, corresponding to the first
sound "A".
The second state is dream, corresponding to the second
sound "U".
The third state is deep sleep, corresponding to the third
sound "M".
Fourth is the state of samadhi, the fully awakened state of
pure consciousness in which our divinity, our unity with
the whole of creation, and with the force behind
creation is recognized. This state is represented by all
three syllables joined together in the one word AUM.'

THE KENA UPANISHAD

The title means 'at whose command'. It begins with some
direct questions, and a statement of the reality behind
appearances.

'By whom is the mind sent forth? What makes life begin?
    What enables me to see, to hear, to speak, to under-
    stand?'
'It is the ear beyond ear,
Eye beyond eye,
Life beyond life.
    The wise realize this "beyond", and attain to
    immortality.
Not what the eye sees,
But that whereby the eye sees.
Not what the ear hears,
But that whereby the ear hears.
And not what the mind thinks,
But that whereby the mind thinks.
    Know this to be Brahman, the spirit. That is not
    Brahman
    Which is studied and worshipped by men.
If you think you know Brahman that very thought means
    that you do not know.
Brahman is beyond knowing, even beyond existence itself.
Only by a sudden flash of realization can Brahman be
    comprehended.
    To achieve this realization meditate continually on
    Brahman.
    Practise austerity, practise self-control.
    Do your duty without attachment, and study sacred
    works,
You must become pure to receive this realization.'

These excerpts from the ten principal upanishads give some
indication of the clarity and freshness of these ancient
teachings. It will be seen as our history progresses how many
of the seed ideas contained in these writings have formed the
basis of important schools of thought later on. These ideas
are still as alive today as they were in ancient India.

CHAPTER 3
Jainism

The Upanishads were like a breath of fresh air blowing through the stuffy corridors of power of Vedic Brahminism. They were noticed by the Brahmin establishment because the yogis did not owe allegiance to any established religion or mode of thought. The free-thinking yogis were tolerated, and even looked up to by some of the more enlightened Brahmins. They appear always to have enjoyed this status among the populace. Their independence and lack of organization has been one factor in the survival of yoga. Efforts to organize it in the past have always failed because organization is contrary to its true spirit.

So although the Upanishads came to be noticed by the Brahmin establishment they were very largely saying what may well have been current among other Sramanic groups at the time. From this unorthodox stream two disciplines were exerting considerable influence, which would continue for a long time thereafter. These were the Samkhya philosophy and the Jain religion. We shall look at the Samkhya philosophy in more detail when we consider the Six Systems of Philosophy, but it can be said now that this atheistic doctrine was evidently very acceptable to the authors of the Upanishads, who made use of many of its concepts. Indeed Samkhya and yoga have been bracketed together when the philosophical aspects of yoga have been under discussion, and they were coupled in the Six Systems, as we will see later on.

Many of the ideas in the Upanishads were also found in Jainism, which appears to have been active at the same time, but was waiting for Mahavira to revitalize it. Jainism, Samkhya and yoga have many ideas in common as we shall see. Tracing the interweaving of these three disciplines throughout this early historical period is extremely interesting and rewarding.

Mahavira has been given the credit as founder of Jainism,

but he merely provided it with a new dynamism. We have already said that their tradition speaks of twenty-three earlier patriarchs, jinas or tirthankaras, as the leaders were generally known. The first was Risabha, the twenty-third Parsva, who lived two hundred and fifty years before Mahavira, a time which would make him contemporary with the early Upanishads. It is to Parsva that Jains of the present day look as the true founder of Jainism.

As always with religious figures, fact tends in time to give way to legend, and Parsva is no exception. He is described as a tirthankara or crossing-maker, that is, one who has crossed to the farther shore. This symbolism of making the crossing of the sea of life and all its illusions to the farther shore of realization occurs time and time again in Indian thought. Even a thousand years later the concepts reappear in the major symbolism of the Mahayana school of Buddhism, when they refer to Mahayana as the larger vehicle or ferry boat that will carry the devotees to the farther shore of nirvana.

Parsva was said to have lived eighty-four thousand years after his predecessor Bhagawan Aristanemi. Legends of Parsva state that he was the son of King Asvasena and his wife Vama. Everyone marvelled at the strength and beauty of the child as he grew up. The delights and temptations of the palace did not interest him. All he wanted to do was to renounce the world, which he eventually did. Many picturesque legends about Parsva and the evil brother of his ninth incarnation are still popular in India. The enmity of his brother continues through various later incarnations, the brothers living human, animal and heavenly lives. These legends show not just the strength of Jain attachment to the idea of reincarnation, but also to their belief that the reincarnating soul can take on animal and angelic bodies as well as human.

Parsva was reputed to have lived exactly one hundred years. For almost seventy years he taught and finally came to Sammeda Hill, still sacred to the Jains. Here the eighty-five ties associated with the four modes of destructive karma were annihilated, and he died in great peace. There are some remarkable parallels between the life and previous incarnations of Parsva and the Buddha, indicating a tradition in India that the early Buddhists were happy to make use of when the time came to invest their saviour with godlike qualities. Even statues of the two are remarkably alike and many a traveller has mistaken their identity. The first of the Jain saviours or crossing-makers is said to have been Rsabanatha, who lived hundreds of thousands of years before. This reputed antiquity matches Buddhist stories of former Buddhas, who were also said to have lived immense ages ago.

Mahavira himself was born at Vaishali, twenty-seven miles north of Patna. He was born of non-Aryan stock, and was a member of the kshatriya caste. He joined the Jain order as a monk, and spent twelve years in self-mortification and the utmost austerity. After thirteen months of the twelve years he discarded his clothing along with all other possessions, and continued to teach for the rest of his life. He had eleven disciples, and finally achieved kevala – release or realization. He died at Pava, aged seventy-two, in 476 BC.

Unlike Brahminism, Jainism has always had monasteries for those who wish to retire from the world. In fact the monasteries could be regarded as the centre and nucleus of the order. The monks practise bodily restraint, chastity, abstinence from alcohol, flesh and honey. The disciplines include raja yoga, purity of thought, meditation and confession. Of their five vows the first and strictest is non-violence. This anticipates Patanjali's Yoga Sutras which appeared later, where non-violence is the first of the yamas or restraints. Their heavy emphasis on the practice of non-violence has led to the distinctive behaviour for which they are famous. They wear a face mask to avoid breathing in insects, and carry a brush to avoid treading or sitting on any living thing.

The monasteries are not separate from the Jain community. The laity are fully involved, and one of its strengths is that lay members will adopt as many of the practices of the monks as are compatible with daily life. There is no priesthood as such.

The Jains hold strongly to the ideas of reincarnation and karma. They hold the view of an ascending order of creation. Rocks, and other apparently lifeless things, do in fact have life however humble, and the souls in them can progress to the very highest states over aeons of time. Souls can change as the bodies they occupy can change. So there is spiritual evolution for the whole of life. Souls possess intelligence, which is indestructible.

According to the Jain view, on reaching human birth a soul can be of two kinds, either liberated or mundane. The latter is subject to rebirth. The former on death becomes disembodied as far as earthly life is concerned and goes on to life in the angelic and other realms. Into each mundane soul pours eight kinds of matter, which is converted into karma. This karma combines with the soul to form a subtle body which determines the spiritual state of the person at that time. As old karma is eliminated new karma comes in, but if the soul is really making progress the new karma will be more subtle, and eventually even that new accretion will come to an end. The teachings are that the soul can enter five stages according to the strength of karma. The character of the soul can be seen by presence or absence of six transcendental colours, three good and three bad. We shall go more fully into the Jain philosophy later, but look first a little further at its history and practice.

The teachings of Parsva and Mahavira are the same, for Mahavira was faithful to the tradition. He never claimed to have founded a new doctrine. What he did was to achieve the full enlightenment of which the tradition speaks. By achieving kevala he became a tirthankara. They speak of a whole series of Jain saviours or tirthankaras going back over hundreds of thousands of years, and emphasize the rarity of kevala's achievement. In fact their teachings are that no more tirthankaras will be born, as the disciplines are too exacting for present-day bodies. This is illustrated in their statues, which are colossal. They depict the various tirthankaras of an earlier golden age, when everybody was big and strong. As moral stamina has declined so has human size. The earth will become progressively more violent and bestial. Yet the continual round of death and rebirth will go on, even in the heavenly realms. Only a tirthankara can release himself from it. The Jains, like the Buddhists, consider that final release is possible only in a male body. Again, like the Buddha, Mahavira never quite accorded women equal status, even though they are allowed to take the same vows as the monks.

An interesting feature of the Jain statues is that though naked, they were deliberately designed to be non-sensual. This is in keeping with those of them who even to this day go 'sky-clad' or naked.

After Mahavira the Jains split into two factions. These are known as Digambaras formerly known as Botikas, and the Svetambharas formerly known as Ardhophalakras. The latter got their name from their white clothes, as distinct from the Digambaras, who followed Mahavira's example and went naked. The Svetambharas claim to be the main group, with the Digambaras formed three years later. Both orders claim allegiance to the sixth patriarch Bhadrabaku, who led many of his followers to the south. Chandragupta Maury abdicated his throne in order to join them. Bhadrabaku also led a vigorous expansion into the north and north-west of India as far as Orissa. Inscriptions have been found on ashoka pillars, proving the Jain presence in that area.

About AD 1125 the king of Gujerat was converted to Jainism, which resulted in considerable expansion in west India, where the Jains are still strong to this day. In the north the Svetambharas set up several schools, the most famous being Upakesa, which is followed by the Oswal Jains. The great age of Jain expansion has left a most valuable legacy of stupas, cave temples and stone carvings. The best examples are found in the south, as many in the north were pillaged by the Moslem invaders who used the stone to build their own mosques. Those in the south contain colossi of the Digambara saint Gomata, or Gomateshvara. The Brahmins caused the destruction of many Jain temples in Delhi and north India, using Ajayapala, as their agent.

Turning to the actual teachings of Jainism we see, first of all, that they view the universe as a vast living organism. It has no beginning, and will have no end. It is animated by life-monads, which pervade the whole of it – humans, animals, all living things, and even rocks. These life-monads are imperishable. We ascend and descend through various forms of life, passing from one state to the next. Only by the perfected seer is the process fully understood.

The life-monads of the highest state of being possess five faculties. These are thinking (manas), span of life (ayus), physical strength (kaya-bala), speech (vacana-bala) and respiration (svasocchvasa-bala). In Samkhya as also in yoga there are five senses – touch, smell, taste, hearing, sight. There are also five faculties of action. These are speech (vaca), grasping (pani), locomotion (pada), excretion (payu) and reproduction (upastha). In the Samkhya yoga scheme manas is linked with buddhi (intuitive intelligence), and with ahamkara (ego consciousness). Also added are the five pranas or life breaths. The historical evidence is that Samkhya and yoga both appear to have built on the much earlier Jain scheme. We have already said that the life-monad is not to be looked on as an individual atom, but something that suffuses the whole living universe, nevertheless it appears as six colourings. These are white (sukla), yellow and rose (padma), red (tejas), dove-grey (kapota), dark blue (nila) and black (krsna). They are grouped in three pairs corresponding to the three gunas of the Samkhya and yoga schemes. The first two colours are sattvic, the second two are rejasic and the third two are tamasic.

One of the hardest of Jain teachings is that the tirthankara, or crossing-maker, eventually goes beyond humanity. In the drive towards enlightenment the very last item of humanity is rejected. Even pity and compassion are left behind, because nothing concerning humanity is his concern any more. In spite of this apparent lack of compassion the tirthankara is still a saviour of humanity; he may even be a saviour of the gods, angels of the realms of heaven. The perfected being can stand apart from human life because he sees it as a picture show. Though all are busy they are only doing what has always been done before. The perfected being therefore has no plans or projects, no ambitions or desires and no personality. He just is.

Jainism shared the general Sramanic view of the universe, and indeed of the whole of existence as God: a kind of pantheism. They took ultimate reality out of the time stream, declaring that the universe had never had a beginning, and will never have an end. This pre-Vedic, pre-Aryan view overcomes the problem of time which is such a stumbling block for Brahminism, and for the Semitic religions of Judaism, Christianity and Islam. All of them conceive of God as an anthropomorphic being who created the world at a particular moment of time. This dualism makes the universe something separate from God, and mankind has seen it as giving him dominion over it, with a licence to exploit the world as he wishes, as long as God is not offended. The earlier Sramanic teachings kept mankind close to earth and taught him to treat the earth and all things in it as he would himself. This view has survived in Jainism to a remarkable degree. The Sramanic disciplines did not feel the need to posit the idea of God at all.

In Jainism the life-monad (jiva) is different from karmic matter (ajiva). This dualism again, seems to anticipate the Samkhya and yoga ideas of purusha (spirit) and prakriti (matter). All posit the idea that before existence was non-existence, which was not void. It was prana (energy). In Jainism every act produces karma. The process of living is by definition the process of producing karma. The karma is of the six colourings, making it good or bad, and determines the course of life thereafter. The life-monad carries an accumulation of good and bad karma in the same way that the brain carries an accumulation of memories, some happy, others unhappy. This karma produces the circumstances of the next life, including physique, appearance and mental capacity.

We are continually emptying ourselves of old karma, and filling ourselves with new. The object of Jain asceticism is to fill only with good karma. The Jains use the analogy of the crystal. In its pristine state it is shining, colourless and transparent. As new karma enters in the form of the six colourings, the colour changes. The colour of the crystal changes throughout life as the karmic debt changes.

This ethical doctrine seems to have been fairly common among all the Sramanic disciplines in pre-Vedic times, but has come down to us in its clearest form with the Jains. The doctrine of karmic colours (lesyas) is not confined to the Jains, and the same simile of the tainted crystal has come down through other cultures to the present day. They claim that a perfected individual can actually see the karmic colours in the human aura. Today many clairvoyants claim to see them. According to the Jains a process of actual physical cleansing takes place by the practice of non-violence, asceticism and deep meditation. When the adept achieves final release all karmic colours leave the crystal, even the brightest, and what is left is pure radiant white light.

Jainism is concerned to restore the life-monad to its pristine purity by kevala (kaivalya in yoga), the process of integration of all elements within the Self. This allows great powers latent in man to become manifest by removing all hindrances. Here again is a faint echo of the nine hindrances listed by Patanjali in the Yoga Sutras. This doctrine of the removal of hindrances became part of Brahminism in the first century AD. The Jain view was rather mechanical compared to the Samkhya yoga, and later Brahminical views.

The Jain view of moksa (release) is also rather mechanical and materialistic, when explaining the processes of the life-monad and the karmic flux. In the Upanishads and in Buddhism an immaterial, psychological outlook is presented. This affects the moral code. In yoga, and later in Buddhism, the intention not to do harm is paramount. In Jainism one must go to great lengths never actually to inflict harm by breathing in, or stepping on, other forms of life. If a Jain destroys another form of life by accident his karmic debt is increased, although he had no harmful intention. The crystal of the life-monad according to the Jains is stained and coloured by all bad karma, so every door through which bad karma can enter must be tightly closed.

Unfortunately such a philosophy has a reductionist effect, so eventually the devotee abstains from action of any kind, knowing that to do so will only make fresh karma. Asceticism becomes progressively more severe, and finally leads to total inaction. This denial of basic humanity is one reason why Jainism has never grown like Buddhism or yoga, both of which allow full play of human emotional warmth, and even sensuality, as long as the intentions are pure. The end for the Jain devotee still in the flesh is to become a jivanmukti, one who is released, but still living out the last remaining traces of karma. He has no further interest in anything, and by the same token is usually ignored or considered an oddity by others.

Some of the rather mechanistic ideas in Jainism came in for heavy criticism by Buddhism. The Buddhists teach that the

intention not to do harm is sufficient, and reject as materialistic errors the idea of the imperishable crystal of the life-
monad and karmic influx. Canonical texts of Buddhism of the
first century BC refer frequently to the Jains as rivals, and
describe them as nirgrantha (demons). In spite of this
opposition Buddhism and Jainism are very similar. Both are
atheistic, and both see the world as a place of suffering, and in
their separate ways prepare their followers to escape from it.
Western scholars, writing from a Christian background, have
labelled them both as pessimistic. The Christian doctrine of
Christ as saviour, and God as a kindly anthropomorphic
entity who always loves us is no doubt how many of us would
like things to be, but the Jain and Buddhist views are more
realistic.

We have already considered the Jain simile of the crystal.
Another is that of the released life-monad, which is likened to
a bubble, rising to the surface of the water. Ascending it
retains its identity as a bubble but when it reaches the surface
it bursts, disappears and ceases to exist. The texts speak of the
enlightened ones as rising to the ceiling of the world. This, of
course, was in the days before we understood the physical
nature of the solar system.

Among their symbols we have already mentioned the
collossal naked male statues, with their deliberately non-
sensual design. These figures are entirely ascetic. Their
female figures on the other hand have affinities with the
mother-goddesses of the neolithic age. They are deliberately
sensual, seeming to indicate that to the Jains this was the
proper function of womanhood. Many of these figures are
indistinguishable from some Hindu statues.

The Jains taught that the universe is a living thing, just like
a human body. This concept of the living universe with its
various functions was not confined to the Jains, but was part
of the whole Sramanic philosophy. As every single part of it is
sacred, and worthy of reverence, even down to rocks and soil,
one must not do violence to any of it. So the Jain monk moves
deliberately, and treads everything gently.

According to the Jains the universe has six constituents:

1   Jiva, the life-monad, or an aggregate of countless life
    monads.

2 Ajiva, what is not, space.
3 Dharma, medium of movement, water, air etc.
4 Adharma, medium of immobility, earth etc.
5 Kala, time.
6 Pudgala, matter in six degrees of density.

Karmic matter clings to the jiva in eight ways:

1 Jnana-avarana-karma, which veils true knowledge.
2 Darsana-avarana-karma, which veils true perception.
3 Vedaniya-avarana-karma, which creates pleasant and
   unpleasant feelings.
4 Mohaniya-avarana-karma, which creates confusion and
   delusion.
5 Ayus-karma, which determines the length of life.
6 Nama-karma, which establishes individuality, and determines present appearance and personality. It is
   analysed into ninety-three sub-divisions.
7 Gotra-karma, which determines the family and circumstances in which one will be born.
8 Antaraya-karma, which produces obstacles. There are
   five sub-divisions mostly to do with pride, which makes
   us refuse help, or to be incapable of enjoyment.

Altogether one hundred and forty-eight varieties and
effects of karma are described. They work in two directions.
The first is ghati-karma, concerned with actively harming.
The second is aghati-karma, which adds limiting qualities not
really part of it. Our bondage is due to identifying jiva with
ajiva. Moksa results when they are separated. This joining
and separation is presented in seven tattvas, or principles.
These are, jiva, ajiva, asrava, the influx of karmic matter into
the monad through forty-two channels, bandha, bondage or
covering the jiva with karmic matter, samvara, or stopping
this influx, nirjara, or elimination of karmic matter, moksa,
release.

According to the Jain cosmology higher beings have ten
faculties:

1 Ayus, life force.
2 Kaya-bala, strength.
3 Vacana-bala, speech.

4   Manobala, reason.
5   Anapana-prana, breath.
6   Sparsendriya, touch.
7   Rasendriya, taste.
8   Ghranendriya, smell.
9   Caksurendriya, sight.
10   Sravanendriya, hearing.

The lowest forms of life have some of these faculties. The higher forms such as man have all of them.

This elaborate system is subtle, and points to a long tradition in which such a minute classification has been built up. The basic dualism of Jainism consists in the formula that jiva and ajiva together make up the whole of existence. The Jains have nothing to say about the origins of the universe, because they do not believe it had a beginning. It has always existed, and always will. Their whole philosophy points to the final release of the life-monad, which on its release becomes omniscient. It sees the truth of everything, and is all-powerful, but never uses this power in the worlds of samsara. They no longer concern it.

The Jains also hold the view in common with both Brahminism and the older Sramanic teachings that personality is a mask to be put on and taken off. It is not real as the basic monad or spirit is real. The Western view, which seems to be shared by the Chinese, is of the personality as a continuing entity, either going on to live in heaven after death, or constantly returning to earth in the process of reincarnation. The idea of reincarnation, so central to the older Sramanic creeds, is still quite new to many people throughout the world. The Aryans of the Vedic age knew nothing of it. When the Brahmins began to accept it they declared it to be a secret doctrine. No doubt they wished to keep it secret from the common people, but the teachings were already being promulgated by the Jains, Samkhyans, and yogis, and were really common knowledge. The one restriction imposed by the yogis was that the doctrine should only be imparted by a guru to those adopting an ascetic and non-violent way of life.

It will be seen from this short account of the Jains that they had fully developed the ideas of reincarnation and karma very early in history. The earliest Upanishads were probably strongly influenced by their teachings. Along with the yogis they practised austerity and meditation. Their extreme non-violence and asceticism has militated against wide acceptance of their teachings, but like yoga it is obvious that they have worked like a leaven in the religious and cultural life of India. Jainism, the religion, Samkhya, the philosophy, and yoga, the way to self-discipline and enlightenment dominated the spiritual life of India in Dravidian times. They were to be overshadowed for a thousand years by the lower form of religion that was foisted on the local inhabitants by the invading Aryans, but in the end it was the Sramanic disciplines which triumphed. They did so by surviving in their own right, and by their ideas becoming fully adopted by the Brahmins who steadily modified their own vedic religion. Yoga fully acknowledges its debt to Jainism, and Jainism reciprocates by making the practice of yoga part and parcel of its spiritual life.

CHAPTER 4
Buddhism

Contemporary with Mahavira was the Buddha, Gotama Sakhyamuni, or Siddhartha Gotama of the Sakhya clan. He was born in 563 BC, left home at the age of twenty-nine, attained enlightenment at thirty-five, and was eighty years old when he died.

Gotama has been described as the greatest of all yogis. Certainly when he left the palace at the age of twenty-nine he took up a strictly yogic way of life, and his meditations and their results were to have a decisive influence on the course of history in the east. Yet one could ask, where would Buddhism be today without the Emperor Ashoka? Again, from the Buddha's own teaching on the path to Buddhahood, why did conscience not strike him until the age of twenty-nine, when he turned his back on the dissolute life of the palace, a life of luxury which he had enjoyed as a right by being a son of the head of the Sakhya clan? Would he have listened to it if he had been born into more humble circumstances?

According to the Buddha's own teachings a male child about to enter his last incarnation would be born virtually spotless, and his own life would have been the same. One thinks of later great yogis such as Sankara and more recently Ramakrishna and Yogananda, who could not touch meat, participate in any violence whatsoever, and according to reliable testimony were in every way chaste and virtuous.

Many tales are told of the birth and early life of Gotama. These are the Jataka tales. Delightful and mostly legendary they suitably mythologize and embellish the circumstances of his birth and his early life. He had a son, Rahula, of whom nothing is known apart from another meeting with him in later life. At this meeting Rahula asked for his birthright, and in response the Buddha enrolled him in the order of monks. We are not told whether this is what the son intended.

When Gotama left his wife and son and the life of the court he took the yoga path of austerity, non-violence and meditation. He became a wandering mendicant as so many had done before him and have done in India right down to the present day. Like the other wandering mendicants he was looking for a guru, a teacher. His first choice was Alara Kalanca. He stayed for some time but was not satisfied with the teaching. He moved on and came to his second guru Udraka. Again he stayed for a while, but again was disenchanted. Neither their teachings nor their examples satisfied him.

So he travelled throughout the kingdom of Magadha, between Benares and Nepal. He came to the town of Uruvela, and there stayed for six years, practising the utmost austerities, and going deeper and deeper into the meditative states. Towards the end of this period he was very near death's door, such were the deprivations he had voluntarily suffered. At this point he decided that for him there could be no release or realization this way. He bathed, clothed himself and began to eat properly again.

During his time in Uruvela he was not alone. He had five companions. They were all mendicants like himself and had kept him company in the same spiritual pilgrimage. When he made his decision to give up the way of austerity they all protested and eventually left him in disgust. They were later to become his first disciples. Now in a more comfortable situation, and presumably a more relaxed state of mind, Gotama again took up his meditations.

Now it was that he received his great enlightenment. To anyone familiar with mystical experience Gotama's sudden enlightenment immediately after his repudiation of austerity will be readily understandable. Severe austerities undoubtedly prepare the body, mind and spirit for the experience, but it is only after relaxing from them that the psyche is released into a new freedom. This mental process happens in much more humble endeavours, as many of us could testify from our own experience. Someone with a problem may leave it and take up something else. As a result and quite suddenly the answer may come. This is what happened with Gotama.

What was the enlightenment that he received? Nowhere in his utterances did Gotama describe the nature of his experience and, surprisingly, it seems that nobody asked him, if we may judge by the accounts that have come down to us. Perhaps in those days there was no deep investigation of mystical experiences. Today nothing is sacrosanct, and everything is closely analysed, even such subtle and highly subjective experiences as the mystical state.

The direct result of Gotama's enlightenment was a startlingly clear statement of the doctrine which was to form the foundation of Buddhism, and which for the rest of his life he would elaborate and embellish. He went to the deer park known as the Jeta Grove at Benares, and there met his friends, the five mendicants who had shared his earlier austerities and meditations. To them he preached his famous sermon, sometimes known as the sermon at Benares, but in his own words, the sermon of the turning of the wheel of the Dharma. This we quoted in full in the introduction. All five mendicants were converted there and then, and became his first disciples.

After his first sermon Gotama wandered about the kingdom of Magadha gathering converts as he went. These converts were instructed to spread the message in their turn. Thus unlike Hinduism, or indeed any of the religions then current in India, Buddhism was from the start a missionary religion.

What exactly was the message of Gotama? We have already seen that certain ideas were well developed in the Upanishads and Jainism. These were the process of reincarnation, and karma, its complementary process. Karma had been greatly elaborated by the Jains, while reincarnation had received clear expression in the early Upanishads. The twin doctrines of reincarnation and karma were therefore fairly common currency at the time of Gotama, and there is nothing original in his adoption of these teachings.

The doctrine of non-violence (ahimsa) has also been elaborated, and applied to an extreme degree by the Jains. These practices were common among all the free-thinkers of the Sramanic stream; so again the picture of the compassionate Buddha, though attractive, was not original. The decisive originality of the Buddha, and the doctrine that was to bring hope and inspiration to millions was that of dukkha – the cause and elimination of suffering. Gotama said, 'I teach of suffering, and the end of suffering. Birth is suffering, decay is suffering, disease is suffering, death is suffering, association with the unpleasant is suffering, separation from the pleasant is suffering, not to get what one wants is suffering.'

He went on to declare the four noble truths about suffering. The first truth is the reality and all-pervading character of suffering. Wherever we turn we cannot escape it. We can observe it in others, and in other forms of life. We suffer continually ourselves. Much of our time is spent restructuring our lives to avoid it. We know what caused our suffering before, so now we make changes to ensure that the same thing does not happen again. Or we escape from it in fantasy by reading novels, watching television or taking up some other opiate. Almost every adult can testify to the reality of suffering. They are fortunate indeed who do not suffer at all.

The second noble truth is that suffering has a cause. To the millions who suffer and have suffered it comes as quite a revelation to realize that, barring accidents, suffering does have a single identifiable cause. The cause is desire. This apparently simple concept is on close examination enormously complex, and takes us into many issues of ethics and morality. There is obviously a world of difference between a desire for wealth and fame, and a desire to free animals from zoos, or from the laboratories of vivisectors. The desire for fame and wealth is highly personal and selfish, the desire to liberate animals is entirely altruistic. The ambitious man will suffer from himself, as the Buddha also said. The altruist will accept suffering in the course of doing his spiritual duty.

The Sanskrit word for what the Buddha meant is trishna (or in Pali, tanka). A highly altruistic desire such as that to free all animals in the vivisection laboratories is not what is meant by trishna. It might be thought that what is meant is selfish desire, but even this is not correct. A person who is deprived in some way could have an earnest, indeed an obsessive desire to end his deprivation, an entirely acceptable desire.

What is meant by trishna is the type of desire or craving which strengthens the ego, causing it to deny its linkage with other human beings, and with the whole of creation. Its opposite is the mystical state, or samadhi according to yoga, in which the overwhelming emotion is a feeling of union with the whole of creation. Between these two extremes we live out our lives. There is a state of tension between them which has to be accepted as part of living. To counteract backsliding into selfishness, and strengthening of the ego that Buddhism is anxious to avoid, all religious and ethical systems by their rituals and writings direct their followers to the opposite virtues.

The third noble truth proclaims that suffering can have an end, and leads on to the fourth truth which is the way to end it. This fourth truth is the noble eightfold path. This path consists in right understanding, right thought, right speech, right conduct, right means of livelihood, right effort, right concentration and right contemplation. When we look at the eight we are struck by an almost total lack of moralizing. The prohibitions of the Judaic/Christian/Islamic ten commandments are missing. What the Buddha is teaching is self-effort, not self-denial. It is positive rather than negative, 'thou shalt' rather than 'thou shalt not'. He is showing the way of jnana yoga in right understanding, of raja yoga in right thought, speech, mind control and meditation and of karma yoga in right livelihood and right effort. His often repeated injunction was to work out your salvation with diligence. The yoga way of self-effort is continually insisted on by Gotama.

Some later sayings attributed to the Buddha are moralizing and list many abstentions. We wonder how genuine they are, since his sayings were not written down until four hundred years after his death. It is always the case that the initial impetus of the founder of any new movement proves to be rather extreme to later followers, who feel happier with less demanding ordinances. Surprisingly enough it is easier to take the path of abstinence than to take the yogic path of self-effort, and self-motivation. The rather lengthy lists of abstentions required of monks might well have been imposed by older monks and not by Gotama.

The subsequent history of Buddhism after the death of the founder shows a more or less continuous process of backsliding. Early Buddhism, known as southern or Theravada, and also known as Hinayana, adopted a more or less moral-istic stance, albeit a very elevated one.

The stages of the eightfold path have been much com-mented on down the ages. Interpretations are personal, and can be highly individual. Most commentators have looked on the eight as moral precepts, but the Buddha stated very specifically that it was a path. In this case one could look for some progression along it. It is possible to see the progression from the point of view of a practising yogi. Right understand-ing must come first. It involves study and thinking round the situation. Disciplined thinking round the situation is right thought. Right speech, conduct and livelihood follow nat-urally as outward manifestations of the effort that has been put into studying and thinking round the situation. Right concentration moves imperceptibly into right contemplation. This last stage leads straight to nirvana or samadhi. In fact the eightfold path when looked at as a path, a progression, is strikingly similar to the eight limbs of yoga as formulated later by Patanjali.

We ask again what is the distinctive message of Buddhism? Every religion and occult tradition has certain hard sayings, teachings that cause us disquiet, or shock us. Buddhism has one such, and it has been the subject of anguished discussion ever since. This is anatta, the doctrine that man has no permanent soul. The Buddha taught that the ego that enables us to live in the world as a self-conscious being is made up of the five skandas, or five grasping principles. These are body, feelings, perception, mentality and consciousness. We cling to these in the belief that they represent the true essence of our being. But if by treading the eightfold path we transcend these we realize in the state of samadhi (nirvana) that they progressively drop away, and we are left with nothing. This nothing is void (sunyata). It is nothing as far as we are concerned, yet it lives.

This apparently contradictory idea takes some understand-ing, but one is helped by realizing that all five skandas are in a continual state of change. As such they can have no perma-nent existence. What we have to avoid is identifying ourselves with them. We need to understand the distinction between the ego and the soul. The ego, which is our consciousness of our own individuality, is constantly changing. But get behind the ego by realizing nirvana, and we realize that the soul is pure and unsullied by any of the five skandas.

The Buddha has also troubled his followers by failing to answer four questions. These are:

1 Whether the universe is eternal or not.
2 Whether the universe is finite or not.
3 Whether life can exist without the body.
4 Whether a Buddha exists after death.

By remaining silent the Buddha was again leading his followers in the direction of self-effort. If people wish to ask these questions then they must make the effort by meditation to find the answers themselves. If he had answered these questions his answers would undoubtedly have been considered authoritative, and further effort by his followers would not be made. In many of his discourses he dismissed such speculations as belonging to a lower order of enquiry.

In a similar way he 'maintained a noble silence' when asked if there was a God. He obviously did not intend bedevilling true religion with theological disputation, the cause of so much misery in the West through religious wars, and much amusement later when we are able to study some of the absurd theories put forward about either the existence or the nature of God. Always the Buddha called on his followers 'to be lamps unto yourselves'. He well knew that if offered the slightest encouragement people will quickly turn away from the path of self-effort into disputation and fantasy. Buddhism as taught by Gotama himself was entirely experiential as yoga is. This element was to be lost completely in certain later schools where the devotees, having lost touch with the fountainhead, turned to rituals, priests, saviours and gods.

The Buddha made a very short analysis of the nature of existence in his doctrine of the three signs of being. All forms of life, he said, have three characteristics in common. They are impermanence, suffering and no permanent soul. These three signs of being are everywhere apparent, but we behave as if everything is permanent, and we also try to escape suffering. We create permanent buildings, institutions, habits. We feel that we need them. But to accept the reality of impermanence is to feel free. To know that at any time we can walk away from it all is a liberating thought. Achievement of enlightenment or liberation enables us to accept the reality of impermanence, and not just to accept it, but to know its essential truth. To realize the impermanence of the self is less easy, but this too comes when one has experienced nirvana.

The Buddha left behind him another formula of three. These are the three refuges. They are repeated daily by millions of people throughout the world:

I go for refuge to the Sangha (order of monks).
I go for refuge to the Dharma (the teachings).
I go for refuge to the Buddha (Gotama).

So although the Buddha demanded self-effort and a high moral code he also left behind these three refuges, which have been the comfort and solace of his followers ever since.

Gotama, the enlightened one, the Buddha, has been described as the greatest of all yogis. As far as his influence goes we cannot disagree with this view. It was Buddhism that was mainly responsible for taking the practice and teachings of yoga throughout Asia. It is a religion which is still changing and developing, as we will see later. Gotama was also known as Sakya muni – the silent sage. The implication is that the Buddha is the symbol of something beyond what can be said and taught. It has also been pointed out that he was not a religious teacher. He was a healer, who diagnosed the human condition, and prescribed the remedy.

Buddhism teaches that there is an involuntary state of mind which is common to all living creatures. This is the root disease. It is inherent in the instinct for survival, but often works against it. This state of mind is known as avidya – craving. But avidya means more than craving. It also means ignorance, or not knowing. This ignorance is a natural function of the life process. We think that our ideas about things represent ultimate reality, and our life consequently is circumscribed by these ideas. They are creations of the mind, involuntary patterns of seeing things. They are relative, but we see them as unalterable facts of existence. One of Gotama's sayings was that there is no sin, only ignorance.

Buddhism attaches no serious importance to knowledge that attaches men more tightly to the web of life. Knowledge that adds a more comfortable material, or more interesting mental background to existence only contributes additional substance to maintenance of the personality. Buddhism ultimately denies the force and validity of all that can be known.

The doctrine of maya (illusion) is present in all the religions of India, and Buddhism is no exception. The Buddhist doctrine of avidya is very much the same. The life illusion causes us to create our own inner, and from that our outer environment. So the world is being continually produced from our own subconscious minds, and affects us in terms of our emotional commitment to our own imperfections. Our task is to extinguish the life illusion so as to see things as they really are.

At the time of the Buddha religious and metaphysical disputation was very much a factor in Indian life. Even in the villages the local sages representing differing views would argue in public to the great delight and entertainment of the populace. Everybody joined in, although caste distinctions militated against full participation by the lower castes. In the Buddha's time the main contestants for the soul of India were Jainism, Ajivika, Veda and Samkhya. Those who did well in these verbal acrobatics were often suitably rewarded. We have already seen in Brihadaranayaka Upanishad how Vajna-valkya was rewarded by the king with thousands of cows. The Buddha never joined in these disputes. His standpoint was such that he could only see them as enmeshing everybody taking part deeper in maya.

What the Buddha was offering was not an intellectual formulation of the kind that lent itself to intellectual disputation, any more than yoga did. As we have said before it was a medical, or psychiatric diagnosis of the human condition, and one that is largely self-evident. After his death many of his followers joined in with these local tournaments and in the process distorted the original teachings to make them more palatable to the Indian mind. Much of the originality was lost, but because it became acceptable it was able to spread. Eventually the compromises became so widespread that

Indian Buddhism became almost indistinguishable from Hinduism as we shall see later. But meanwhile it began to gather momentum in the land of its birth, and experienced an enormous expansion when the Emperor Ashoka (264–227 BC) became converted.

Ashoka instituted pilgrimages to the various places that were important in Gotama's life. These were the place of birth, the place of death, the place of enlightenment and so on. Ashoka was said to have supported sixty-four thousand monks, erected eighty thousand stupas, and countless monasteries. He also sent Buddhist missionaries to Syria, Egypt, Macedonia and Epirus. His empire included India, southern Afghanistan, Kashmir and Nepal. He ordered a vegetarian diet for everybody, and brought in edicts for the protection of birds and wild animals. Even insects were included. His younger brother Mahendra took the teaching to Sri Lanka, an event of great significance as it was in Sri Lanka that Buddhism survivied when in later times the Brahmin reaction drove it out of India.

CHAPTER 5
The Bhagavad Gita

In the Bhagavad Gita we see Indian capacity for synthesis at its most inspired. In eighteen brief chapters is displayed a kaleidoscopic mingling of the two streams that for over a thousand years had been contending for the Indian mind. It is highly significant that when the synthesis of these two streams did come, it was expressed in almost exclusively yoga terms. The reason is easy to see. The other elements of the Sramanic stream, of which the most important were Samkhya the philosophy and Jainism the religion, were more or less in total opposition to Brahminism. They did not have sufficient flexibility to lend themselves to synthesis. Yoga on the other hand had no intellectual content as such. Its content had been and still is experiential. The mental concepts that had arisen from the meditative and contemplative experiences were self-evident to a very high degree once they had been brought out into the open.

Although both Jainism and Samkhya were atheistic and dualistic yoga had never made a stand either philosophically or religiously. Most of its devotees before Sankara tended to accept the Samkhya philosophy, largely because its main concepts of purusha and prakriti and the three gunas were confirmed by the results of yoga meditation. The principal Jain ideas of reincarnation and karma, and that ultimate reality is outside the time scale, were also ideas borne out by experience in deep meditation.

These Jain and Samkhya ideas had to some extent been already synthesized and restated in the early Upanishads. The Bhagavad Gita took the process a stage further by accommodating the latest thinking in the new Hinduism that was supplanting the older Brahminism, and which was later known as Vedanta. This Vedanta as we have said before was based on the Upanishads, which were added on at the end of the Vedas, 'anta' meaning end. The word Vedanta can also be taken to mean the end of the Vedic age, which the Bhagavad Gita undoubtedly brought in. After the Upanishads and the Bhagavad Gita, the Vedas were largely ignored. Often they were ridiculed. Today they stand as quaint survivals of a lower form of religion, studied only by scholars for their historical interest.

While Jainism and Samkhya were atheistic and dualistic Brahminism was theistic and monistic. The Bhagavad Gita brought these together. Thereafter, and especially after Patanjali and Sankara, yoga devotees tended to become theists and monists also. The Bhagavad Gita made the syntheses by stating that monism explained the ultimate while dualism explained the working of the universe. Just as the many gods of the Hindu pantheon had earlier been demoted as it were in favour of the one God Brahman-Atman, so the two basic elements of the cosmos, purusha and prakriti, were also demoted in favour of the Brahman-Atman equation.

This would seem to indicate a victory for Brahminism over the Sramanic stream, but the truth is that the Brahman-Atman equation was arrived at by the processes of yogic meditation and not by intellection. The yogis bypassed the thinking process by means of introspection and contemplation. The mind was encouraged to go beyond itself into the realm of intuition and integral vision, into an awareness in which the processes of mundane thought were arrested by looking within instead of looking to what is continually presented to the senses from outside.

From the time of the acceptance of the unity of Brahman and Atman and its incorporation into yoga philosophy, the pairs of opposites, of which purusha and prakriti are chief, are seen as abstractions of the intellect. The yoga adepts, through accepting the Samkhya philosophy, had continued their meditations and had already gone beyond it to this further unification. Yoga could be said to have parted company with Samkhya at this point, and through the Upanishads, the Gita, and on through Patanjali and Sankara to have been the principal founders of Vedanta.

It would of course be quite wrong to claim this for yoga alone. The Brahmins had for some time been seeking common ground with the Sramanics. As their gods and rituals became increasingly irrelevant under the metaphysical speculations of the rishis, and as the caste system which maintained so much of their power was under attack from all quarters, including the newly emergent Buddhists, they could already discern the end of an era. Some of the later metrical Upanishads were undoubtedly the work of Brahmins who, taking up the practices of mental yoga, were discovering for themselves new depths of understanding.

So with the Bhagavad Gita we see this co-operation in its fullest form, resulting in this synthesis full of contradictions and inconsistencies, and treasured not just in spite of but because of them, for in this seminal work we see how the Indian mind takes up the new ideas, yet also refuses to relinquish the old. This is the typical Indian syncretism that is the despair of the more rational and logical Western mind. The crude Vedic religion of ritualism, sacrifice and priest-craft here combines with the more ancient, yet more sophisticated thought of the Sramanic stream, and produces an amalgam which was eventually to result in Vedanta and later tantra which remains today. In the Bhagavad Gita the more direct and efficient form of yoga is extolled, while the older and more cumbersome ritualistic forms of Brahminism are also acknowledged as having value for those not able to practice any of the forms of yoga which it advocates.

The Gita is a chapter in the Mahabharata; Maha means great, Bharata is an ancient name for India, so the name means Great India. This enormous epic can be compared to Homer's 'Odyssey' but is many times longer. It depicts the rivalries of two clans, the Kauravas and the Pandavas. They are blood relatives, though in opposition. Events culminate in a confrontation, and both clans are drawn up for battle.

Arjuna, the leader of the Pandavas, sees his kinsfolk and friends on both sides and is in great agony of mind. He does not wish to be responsible for the slaughter to come and speaks of his doubts to his charioteer. The charioteer hears him speak and then reveals himself as Krishna, a reincarnation of the Hindu trinity, the gods Brahma the creator, Siva the destroyer, and Vishnu the preserver of the worlds of existence. The dialogue that follows is about dharma or spiritual duty. The Gita is also the first and clearest statement of karma yoga, the yoga of selfless action. This yoga is elaborated in various ways.

The importance of the Gita cannot be over-emphasized. For the first time the practice of yoga is brought right down into ordinary life. A new kind of yoga is promulgated. This is not the traditional ascetic and meditative jnana yoga of the Upanishads, but an active yoga of everyday living. It is not intended to supplant but to complement the older form. Its results are to be social and psychological, not transcendental. The full potential of this yoga has yet to be realized, and the Gita has by no means had the last word.

This yoga of selfless action takes hold of the ancient concept of dharma, and makes its ramifications more understandable to ordinary people. The concept, which is basic to Purva-Mimamsa, one of the Six Systems of Philosophy, is here brought out into the daylight and given a broader interpretation. From being a moral precept it became an active discipline, being combined with yoga in a most original way.

Karma yoga calls for performance of the ordinary activities of daily life, but ordains detachment from their fruits. Think of the act, not the result. In our own times this principle was used by Mahatma Gandhi, who insisted at all times on 'the purity of the means'. Gandhi was referring to the political doctrine that any means to arrive at a desirable end were justified, that violence might be justified in order to gain peace as a result. Gandhi opposed this doctrine, and so would the karma yoga of the Bhagavad Gita.

Krishna pointed out to Arjuna that pleasure and pain, defeat and victory are of equal worth. The wise fulfil the duties of life in a spirit of joyful routine, aware that one cannot escape from it, so why not submit. However mean the work, do it well, without attachment. The work is for perfecting of the soul, so the type of work does not matter.

Krishna also emphasizes the changeless ego. Do not feel pity for those who must die, he says to Arjuna. Pity has no place. The wise feel no pity for what dies or what lives. There was never a time when we were not in existence. Nor will there ever be a time when we will cease to be. Every tissue of the universe is imperishable, and nothing can destroy it.

In the Gita the three gunas are described as proceeding from the Godhead. Brahman-Atman is beyond them. In Samkhya they were part and parcel of the purusha-prakriti ultimate reality. Just as Vedanta incorporated the Hindu gods by postulating one God above them all, so the Gita incorporates Samkhya by the same device. The indestructible life-monad (purusha), according to Samkhya the core and life-seed of each individual, in the composite system of the Bhagavad Gita is but a particle of the one supreme being, with which it is in essence identical. Thus the transcendent monism of Vedanta is reconciled with the pluralistic life-monad of Samkhya. The two systems are now understood as descriptions of the same reality from differing points of view. Vedanta presents the higher truth, Samkhya is an empirical analysis of the logical principle of the lower, rational sphere of the pairs of opposites. In the latter the antagonistic principles are in force which constitute the basis of all normal human experience and rational thought. Dualism belongs to the sphere of manifestation acting through the gunas. Nevertheless because it is logical and accords with the facts of life it is not necessarily consonant with the final truth.

Krishna points out that the supreme being does not try to draw everyone to itself. He permits and takes delight in the many ways and illusions of mankind, and he approves of every kind of faith and creed. He sees mankind wrapped in maya (illusion), subject to the workings of the three gunas, but does not intercede to enlighten them. The whole process is lila (play). Those who worship lower gods go to them at death, but those who worship Krishna will go to him. The gods too are subject to maya and the gunas. Only the absolute Brahman-Atman is beyond them, yet exists in all of them, and in all forms of life.

The Bhagavad Gita is regarded by Hindus as smriti, a teaching transmitted by enlightened rishis, yogis and saints, which explains and elaborates the Vedas and Upanishads. The latter are known as sruti, and are considered to be authoritative doctrines transmitted directly from God to man. The Gita is reputed to have been written by Vyasa, whose dates are unknown. They have not been placed more exactly than between 500 and 200 BC. There are no references to

Buddhism in the Gita, which has led some scholars to consider it pre-Buddhist. Others consider that it may have been composed as part of the Hindu reaction to Buddhism, which had been widely popularized by Emperor Ashoka (264-277 BC). It may have been the Buddhist challenge that impelled the author to attempt this great synthesis, and so present a common front to the common enemy. Incorporation into the Mahabharata ensured its immortality. It could hardly have lived on its own except as a manual for a minority.

The literary form of the Gita is that of a dialogue between Krishna and Arjuna, the very mortal hero who is shortly to lead his people into battle. But there is a third presence. This is Sanjaya, who mediumistically is aware of what is being said in the dialogue, and is transmitting it to King Dhritarashtra. Sanjaya carries the message and occasionally puts in some remarks of his own. So does King Dhritarashtra. We shall look at each chapter in turn, and try to extract the essence of it.

The opening chapter portrays the anguish and agony of mind of Arjuna at the slaughter which is to come. His charioteer then reveals himself as Krishna.

In the second chapter the great theme of dharma is introduced. This important concept, which is more fully elaborated in the Purva-Mimamsa philosophy, appears to have no real parallel with the Semitic religions, whose emphasis is on love, as in Christianity, or obedience, as in Judaisim and Islam. Krishna speaks, and tells Arjuna that his sorrow is misplaced. The truly wise do not mourn for the dead, nor do they show pity for the living. Humanity makes its own karma, and spins its own illusions. Bodies die, but the soul is eternal. The soul is never slain, though its body may be. Death is certain, and rebirth is certain.

Krishna then makes a concession to caste, and points out that as a member of the kshatriya or warrior caste Arjuna has a duty to fight. He then introduces the theme of karma yoga. In this yoga all effort produces good karma. One must overcome the three gunas, and be free from the pairs of opposites. Be tranquil. When established in this state of mind the Vedas are superfluous. When you are free from all delusions you will be indifferent to the results of your actions.

This is the central theme of karma yoga – to work

according to one's dharma, but be unattached to the results of one's works. Be established in the Atman, and walk among sense objects unaffected by them. To find the Atman, control the mind and withdraw the senses. Find the Atman, unite it with Brahman, and then do your duty. In this state of mind your work will be effective, and you will not be anxious about results.

In chapter three the theme is again karma yoga. Action is necessary in the world. In the process of living we are active. We cannot escape from it. We are all ruled by the three gunas. Nevertheless there are those who find enlightenment by knowledge. These are the jnana yogis, and there are those who find enlightenment by the way of selfless action. These are the karma yogis. For them every act is a sacrament.

Krishna points out that though divine, and able to have anything he wants, yet he must continue to act as an example to humanity. If he did not work others would not follow his example and the human race would perish.

In chapter four Krishna introduces the Hindu idea of the avatar, an incarnation of the highest gods, who comes to earth at times of trouble and stress to lead mankind in the right direction. In every age a new avatar appears. He brings an old message, but stated in a way that is relevant to that age, and so understandable by those living at that time. He then turns again to the doctrines of karma yoga. There can be action in apparent inaction, and inaction in apparent action. Only the enlightened can be aware of the true value of action. He then surveys the fields of yoga, making reference to jnana yoga in which senses are withdrawn from sense objects. Others (tantric yogis) do the opposite; they enjoy the senses, seeing Brahman in the whole manifested universe. Others renounce material possessions. Others practise raja yoga. Others (bhakti yogis) practice devotion to a personal god. Some practise breathing and other exercises, and others mortify the flesh or practise extreme asceticism, thus reducing their desires to nothing. All of these ways involve action.

In chapter five Krishna speaks of renunciation by saying that just as we have spoken of performing actions in a selfless way, so one can renounce actions in a selfless way. If a person is without desire he can renounce anything, and not feel impoverished. The enlightened seer established in Brahman will eat and drink, sleep and work, breathe and walk, yet as he does all these things he will be saying all the time, 'I am doing nothing'. While he acts according to his dharma his higher Self looks on and sees it merely as a picture show. His senses, body and intellect, are all really separate from his real Self, which is untouched by them.

Chapter six is about meditation. It begins with Krishna again defining karma yoga. Whoever works according to his dharma but cares nothing for the fruits of his actions is a true yogi. If he is anxious over the future he is no yogi. The yogi views everything equally – all the pairs of opposites. The yogi should live alone in a solitary place, and meditate on the Self unceasingly. The posture for meditation must be motionless, with spine erect and eyes focused at the end of the nose. Yoga is not for him who overeats, or fasts, or sleeps too much. He must be moderate in all things.

The yogi must free himself from all mental distractions fixing his attention only on the Self, the Atman. If the mind wanders it must be drawn back unceasingly. The yogi sees the Self in all things, and all things in the Self. He suffers the sorrow of all creatures, and feels joy at their happiness.

If a man practises yoga, but falls away from the practice, finding it too rigorous he will still have earned merit. He will be born again in better circumstances than his present life. In his next life he will return to the position he reached in this life, and will be able to make further progress. In this way he will reach perfection through many births. The yogi who seeks to unite the Self with Brahman is greater than those who practise austerities. He is greater than the learned, and greater than those who practise good works.

Chapter seven is on Krishna's own nature. Here he speaks of the concepts of prakriti, of the gunas and of maya. Those who take refuge in Krishna will through him discover their inner Self and Brahman, with which it is identical.

Chapter eight speaks of the nature of Brahman. Brahman is not caused by anything. When lodged as the Self of an individual he is called Atman. Really both are identical. They are merely seen from different points of view. I, Krishna, am Atman-Brahman in human form. At the hour of death a man

should think only of me. The last thing that one thinks about
at death will be the thing that was uppermost in his mind
during life. The last thought will carry over at death to
comfort or torment him in the paradise realms between death
and rebirth. Therefore concentrate on me, and you will come
to me.

Meditate on me, and use the sacred syllable AUM to aid
your meditation. Use this syllable at the time of death.
Whoever comes to me does not return to rebirth in this life.
There are two paths. The first is Deva-Yana, the path of the
bright ones which leads to higher worlds. The second path is
Pitriyana, the path that is subject to space and time, and leads
back to rebirth. Choose your path Arjuna, and tread it to the
end.

Chapter nine speaks of the mystical state of union with
Brahman. All creatures exist within me, within Brahman. In
the nights of Brahman all creation and manifestation is drawn
to a close. In the days of Brahman all creation and manifestation is opened again. The cycle is repeated over immense
aeons of time. All the multitudes of beings are helpless to
arrest this process. Maya veils reality from all of them. I am
everything that man can conceive of. Everything in manifestation. Do not just worship one of my thousand forms or
faces. Worship me at the centre of your being.

All can come to me. There are no distinctions of race or
sex. The four castes, brahmins, kshatriyas, vaishyas, sudras,
even the outcastes – all can come to me, instantly if their
hearts are pure and their concentration one-pointed.

Chapter ten is a hymn of praise to Atman-Brahman and
Krishna as their human form. Starting with the origin, this
paeon of praise goes on to extol the multitudinous manifestations of this godhead in all walks of life, in all activities, all
forms of religion and worship, and all forms of action and
endeavour.

Chapter eleven reveals the divine form of the godhead in
all its majesty. Arjuna beholds the entire universe in all its
manifold diversity concentrated in a single being before him.
Krishna exhorts Arjuna to go into battle and the day will be
his, and then reappears in human form.

Chapter twelve speaks of bhakti yoga; the yoga of love and devotion. The jnana yogis worship the manifest god which is beyond thought, and indefinable. But their way is difficult, and is only for the minority. Others may better approach god by worshipping it as Krishna in human form, with qualities of goodness, mercy and compassion. They can approach him by concentrating on him. If this is too difficult let them offer their works to him. If this is too difficult then they may surrender themselves completely to him, controlling all desires. Be compassionate to all creatures, and be unmoved by success or failure, by praise or blame. The mind must be fixed only on Atman-Brahman manifested in human form as Krishna.

Chapter thirteen speaks of prakriti and Brahman. Prakriti is matter, the whole of the universe. The body is also prakriti. Through the body we sow karma to be harvested in due course. But beyond prakriti is Brahman. Prakriti issues forth from Brahman. So ordinary people and even those who are learned will study the manifold forms of prakriti, but the wise study the stillness at the centre, which is Brahman.

Both Brahman and prakriti have no beginning and are without end. The body and individuality of man proceed from prakriti, and are subject to the three gunas. But the innermost Self, the Atman, is at one with Brahman. It is not of prakriti, nor subject to the three gunas.

Chapter fourteen is about the gunas. When a new day of Brahman begins the enlightened ones have no part in it. They have been released forever from the round of death and rebirth. At the beginning of the new cycle prakriti will be quickened into birth, and the three gunas will begin to operate.

The gunas are sattva, rajas and tamas. Sattva is light, and can reveal the Atman. But it can bind by making one search for happiness, and long for greater knowledge. Rajas is passion and activity. It binds by making one wish for pleasures, and for wealth. Tamas is ignorance, and binds only by sloth, laziness and delusion. In every person one of the gunas dominates over the other two. We tend to yield to whichever is dominant.

Karma is also ruled by the three gunas. The quality of the
karma will issue in forms that are sattvic, rajasic or tamasic.
The fruit of righteous living is sattva, pure joy. The fruit of
riotous living is rajas, pain and sorrow. The fruit of lazy living
is tamas, greater ignorance.

A man has transcended the gunas when he has no longing
for any of them, not even sattva. He rests in the peace of the
Atman. As he cannot cease from activity and therefore from
the generation of further karma, he is watchful over the
karma that he does generate. It is of such a nature that he has
full consciousness of it, and it is completely under his control.

Chapter fifteen opens with a reference to the aswattha tree,
the tree with its roots in heaven, and its branches on the
earth. The symbol is met with earlier in the Upanishads. One
must sharpen the axe of non-attachment to cut through the
aswattha tree, and so become one with Brahman from whom
all activity streams. Yogis who have become tranquil can
understand Brahman within themselves. Others, who lack
tranquillity and discernment can never reach this realization,
however hard they try.

In life there are those beings who are mortal, who return
constantly to rebirth. There are those who are immortal
because they have escaped from rebirth, and there is the
supreme reality Atman-Brahman which is beyond the mortal,
and beyond the immortal.

In chapter sixteen Krishna compares the man of divine and
the man of demonic tendencies, and elaborates on the latter
at length. The man of demonic tendencies is arrogant,
conceited, cruel and ignorant. His birthright is greater
bondage. The demonic do not rightly know how to conduct
themselves. They do not see any moral law in life. They
consider it to have been conceived in lust, and that lust and its
gratification are all-important. They are unceasingly busy
piling up wealth, and treading on others to get it.

Hell has three doors: lust, rage and greed. All three must
be avoided or they will lead you downwards. For one who has
sunk to the lowest depths the way to climb back is first to practise the yoga of selfless action, karma yoga. This is easiest for
them. Then read the scriptures, and so rise to bhakti and the
ascending order of yogas. The task is immeasurably difficult,

and will take many incarnations, and aeons of time.

In chapter seventeen Krishna speaks of religion. A person's faith or form of religion will be followed according to his ruling guna. Men of sattva will worship God as supreme Brahman. Men of rajas will worship power and wealth. Men of tamas will worship the spirits of the dead, and make gods of the ghosts of their ancestors.

The food which is agreeable to these people will also be of different sorts. The men of sattva will have food that is mild, grown in the fresh air and sun-ripened. Men of rajas will have food that is strong tasting, meaty, salty and sour. The men of tamas will take food that is heavy and tasteless, and will enjoy the leavings of others.

When sacrifice is offered by men of sattva it is offered out of duty, and without thought of their own advantage. By men of rajas it is offered in hope of reward. By men of tamas it is offered blindly and resentfully. The men of sattva practise austerity in order to realize Brahman. The men of rajas do it to gain powers of black magic. The men of tamas are totally unable to practise austerity.

Om Tat Sat is a divine formula which designates Brahman in the process of worshipping him. Om is uttered at any time, but especially before any act of worship. Tat is uttered during the act of worship to indicate that the worshipper desires no reward for his worship. Sat is uttered during the act of worship to indicate that all actions are dedicated to Brahman. If any act of worship or any act of meditation is done without concentration on Brahman that act is Asat, unreal. It will not produce any good result.

The final chapter, eighteen, is on the yoga of renunciation. Krishna teaches renunciation and non-attachment. Renunciation is to give up all actions motivated by desire, and non-attachment is to renounce the fruits of the action. Some have declared that all action must be given up. Some that everything should be given up except acts of worship, austerity and meditation. But the fact is that no action can be given up. There must always be action, but the guna which dominates that action must be carefully selected, and be completely known.

If a man renounces actions ordained by the scriptures his

renunciation is inspired by tamas. If a man abstains from an action because it is disagreeable his renunciation is inspired by rajas. But if a man performs an act dictated by the scriptures, however disagreeable, that man is ruled by sattva. No one can give up action, but if the fruits of action are given up that person has achieved non-attachment. He is ready to reach supreme Brahman.

There are three kinds of conscience. It has the nature of sattva when it can distinguish between renunciation and worldly desire. Conscience has the nature of rajas when it cannot distinguish between right and wrong. It has the nature of tamas when so thickly veiled in illusion that it actually mistakes right for wrong.

The determination of sattva never wavers. It is completely controlled. The determination of rajas can be turned aside by some sense object, or some benefit which has come in the way. The determination of tamas is inspired by obstinacy only.

A man may become perfect if he devotes himself to the work that comes naturally to him. His own duty imperfectly done is immeasurably more valuable than the duty of another, however well done. Says Krishna, 'To me you should surrender yourself. To me go for refuge. With me unite yourself, and all your difficulties will be overcome. If you say Arjuna that you will not fight, your own nature will drive you to do it. You have created your own karma. You are helpless in its power, and you will do the very thing that your mind says you will not do.'

Arjuna goes out to fight, and wins the battle.

The Bhagavad Gita transmits the ancient Samkhya philosophy at a very popular level, and invests it with rich meaning. The author combines it with the various yogas, and for good measure adds a new one, karma yoga, the yoga of selfless action. It makes some necessary concessions to the Vedas and to the Brahmins, and popularizes the main teachings of the Upanishads. Finally it brings in the ancient Jain insistence on non-violence and compassion to all living creatures.

The Bhagavad Gita is the prime work both of Hinduism and of yoga. It is as alive today as it was when written by Vyasa between 2,200 and 2,500 years ago.

CHAPTER 6
The Yoga Sutras of Patanjali

The Yoga Sutras have had a most profound effect on the development and practice of yoga ever since they were first penned. They are inspiring, penetrating and concise. They include in their small compass all the main practices of yoga.

Like so much Indian teaching these instructions to would-be yoga devotees are not a fully worked out system. They are mere hints and suggestions. For this reason it has always been customary for teachers to write a commentary on each sutra to amplify or clarify its meaning. As space does not permit me to do this, I have tried to present each sutra and concept so that on a first reading the meaning is clear and immediate. The Sutras are not part of a narrative, or of a developing argument. They are a series of meditations. So to get the most from a reading of them they should be meditated on and read slowly.

No definite date has been arrived at for Patanjali. Some scholars have identified him with the Sanskrit grammarian of the same name, who lived about 300 BC. But there is no proof that he was the same person. He certainly came after the Upanishads and early Buddhism, and probably also after the Bhagavad Gita. That work widely popularized yoga, but makes no mention of Patanjali, nor of the most celebrated parts of the Sutras, the eight limbs of yoga and the idea of samyama. The Bhagavad Gita was concerned with karma yoga, jnana and bhakti yoga. Patanjali's yoga is really raja yoga, the yoga of mental processes, of mind and will power.

The Sutras are a very concise and expert analysis of the human mind, its nature and functions. Patanjali's work deals with the simplest efforts at mental discipline, takes one to the heights of samadhi, and in part three demonstrates how to use the mind as a tool to achieve certain ends.

The book is divided into four sections. Part one deals with

basic principles, part two with the disciplines, part three with miraculous powers, and part four with illumination. The following rendering of the Sutras is the essence distilled from many translations. Whilst the arrangement into four parts is retained I have departed from the usual system of presenting each sutra separately, as this leads to confusion of ideas. There are many anomalies in the original. Patanjali's text was repetitive, often obscure, sometimes inconsistent. Part three is believed by some scholars to have been added or expanded later. So, although I have retained the continuity, the sutras have been grouped to emphasize a particular concept. The repetitions have been eliminated. Where there was obscurity I have tried to clarify the meaning, and to present the main ideas in modern terms in a consistent manner.

PART 1   PRINCIPLES OF YOGA

Sutras 1–11
Raja Yoga is control of thought. When not controlling his thoughts a man remains their slave.
There are five kinds of thought: right understanding, wrong understanding, illusion, sleep and memory.
Right understanding comes by true evaluation, intuition, and study of sacred writings.
Wrong understanding comes by faulty evaluation or presumption.
Illusion is perception with no correspondence in the external world.
Sleep is dissociated thought.
Memory is recall of past impressions.

Sutras 12–16
Thought control comes by practice of detachment.
Practice means repeated effort to follow the disciplines that result in permanent thought control. It must be made over a long period with earnest devotion.
Detachment means deliberately expelling desire for what is experienced.
Uniting or identifying with one's higher Self is the highest form of detachment.
Those who would progress on the path of yoga must possess

confidence, zeal, single-mindedness and diligence.

Sutras 17–29
Concentration on an object progresses through four phases: awareness, discrimination, joyful merging with the object, total identification with it.
Concentration may also be practised without an object. This means watching the random thought waves while practising detachment. Concentration while suspending detachment, and without an object, may bring the aspirant to the mystical experience of union with reality.
Integration may be attained by intense devotion to God.
The sound which expresses God is AUM. It should be repeatedly intoned while absorbing its meaning.

Sutras 30–34
Disharmony in body and mind retards progress, and is manifested in nine ways. They are disease, anxiety, scepticism, vacillation, inertia, self-deprecation, self-glorification, rivalry and lack of concentration.
These nine disharmonies result in pain, grief, fear and spiritual desolation.
They can be removed by physical labour, or by rhythmic breathing.
Harmony is also restored by practice of the virtues of compassion, courtesy, integrity and tranquillity.

Sutras 35–39
Encouragement to the aspirant may come by flashes of extra-sensory perception resulting from his practice.
Guidance to the aspirant may come by inspiration received on waking from deep sleep.
Assistance to the aspirant may come by devotion to a master, either incarnate or discarnate, by contemplation of a divine picture or symbol that inspires him, or by joyful chanting or singing of mantras or sacred tunes.

Sutras 40–51
The yogi contains in his mind reflection of all that is, the immense and the minute.
When the mind is focused clear of the running of random

thoughts, it identifies with the chosen object of concentration. This state is known as samadhi. There is lower and higher samadhi.

Lower samadhi attains identity of mind with object, but awareness of self remains.

Higher samadhi attains identity of mind with object, but self withdraws.

Lower samadhi retains traces of desire and attachment.

In higher samadhi mind is translucent. No thoughts disturb it.

Comprehension by teaching or intuition is good, but awareness attained in samadhi is of a better kind. It is direct experience.

PART 2   DISCIPLINES OF YOGA

Sutras 1–11
Simplicity, study and joyful dedication of labour to forward evolution are the beginnings of yoga.

There are five hindrances to yoga. They are: ignorance, self-aggrandizement, attachment, aversion and self-preservation.

Ignorance is the root cause of all the other hindrances.

Self-aggrandizement causes separation from others by attempting to become their superior.

Attachment is clinging to an object or idea because of the pleasure it gives.

Aversion is rejection of an object or idea because of the pain it gives.

Self-preservation is rejection of an object or idea because of the pain it gives. Self-preservation is instinctive. But even this must be overcome for attainment of full illumination.

The five hindrances are overcome by persistent meditation upon them, so reducing them that they are eventually destroyed. The mind is then free to return to its own true centre.

Sutras 12–17
Adverse habits are initially formed by one or more of the five hindrances. Until destroyed they will continue to produce karma manifested in this or a future life.

So long as cause exists, then effect must follow, either with joy or grief.

Joy and grief are results of either worthy or unworthy actions. But to the enlightened all experience is grievous, even joy, because its cessation is feared.

New karma can be avoided by understanding the hindrances that cause it.

Thus we cease to identify ourselves with the physical body, which is merely a temporary instrument for our use.

Sutras 18–27

Running through all objects and experiences are the three gunas.

They are tamas (inertia), rajas (activity), and sattva (formation).

From their integration all creation has grown, and is sustained.

The gunas extend through the four planes: material, emotional, intellectual, spiritual.

The universe is experienced by the Atman in order to be purified and liberated from it.

The Atman is essential consciousness, the observer beyond mind. It appears to change, but is changeless.

The universe is God manifest. It exists to express the Atman. It is unreal to one who is awakened, but remains real to others. The Atman is identified with the universe so that by discrimination their unity in diversity may be realized.

Identification of the Atman with the universe ceases and discrimination is attained when ignorance is dispelled. With discrimination the Self realizes that it is unique and indestructible.

Discrimination is attained by cultivation of seven qualities: introspection, control, integration, enthusiasm, tolerance, endurance and balance.

Sutras 28–29

By undeviating effort in the eight spiritual practices of yoga man becomes familiar with the Atman.

The eight practices, or limbs of yoga are: yama (restraint), niyama (observance), asana (posture), pranayama (control of prana), pratyahara (sense withdrawal), dharana (concentration), dhyana (meditation), samadhi (realization).

Sutras 30–45
Yama is restraint from harming other living creatures, from falsehood, from theft, from incontinence and from greed. These are the laws of personal conduct.
By restraint from harming others comes universal brotherhood.
By restraint from falsehood comes good karma, even without the performance of good works.
By restraint from theft comes true wealth.
By restraint from incontinence comes spiritual energy.
By restraint from greed comes release from time.
Niyama is observance of cleanliness, contentment, simplicity, study and devotion to God.
By cleanliness comes freedom from sensuality.
By contentment comes true happiness.
By simplicity comes special powers of body, mind and senses.
By study comes our unique apprehension of reality.
By devotion to God comes samadhi.

Sutras 46–55
Asana is an alert yet relaxed posture achieved by physical control combined with meditation.
Pranayama is control of the flow of prana, beneficial to mind and body, by regulation of the breath.
Pratyahara is abstraction of the mind from sense objects. As a result the senses also withdraw. At this level yoga is attained.

PART 3   MIRACULOUS POWERS

Sutras 1–12
The transcendent three of the eight spiritual practices are dharana, dhyana and samadhi.
Dharana is concentration of attention on an object or idea.
Dhyana is meditation on the chosen object or idea continuously.

Samadhi is total immersion of self in the object or idea. The mind is no longer involved in the process. The aspirant becomes the object of his contemplation.

There is graduation from lower samadhi, which is identification, to higher samadhi which is mystical union outside time and space.

When these three practices are collectively applied to an object or idea, and are driven by the power of will the exercise is known as samyama. By samyama the yogi assumes miraculous powers.

These powers are sought step by step, with meticulous and ordered attention to the final three practices: firstly concentration, secondly meditation, thirdly immersion. Lastly, enforced by the will the three are operated together. That is, samyama is worked.

The yogi is one who has mastered the eight spiritual practices, and knows the technique of samyama.

Sutras 13–16

There are three kinds of change working continuously in nature, through all its physical and spiritual forms. They are change of state, change of shape, and change of time.

All things are subject to change. Life is continual renewal. This is the process of evolution.

By samyama on these changes the life processes are understood. The law of karma is recognized. Former incarnations are recollected.

Sutras 17–33

By the practice of samyama all knowledge can be gained.

Samyama on the sound of words and on the emotions evoked thereby brings understanding of the language of all creatures.

Samyama on habits of thought brings insight into the karmic conditions of which each habit was born. This can extend back into former incarnations.

Samyama on the appearance and thought habits of another yields understanding of his conduct.

Samyama on the qualities of light and sight, so that one can diffuse their wavelengths, brings ability to create the illusion of invisibility.

Samyama on the workings of karma and will, either in oneself or another, brings appraisal of the length of the present incarnation.

Samyama on benevolence generates that quality.

Samyama on strength generates strength.

Samyama on one's own consciousness generates cosmic consciousness.

Samyama on the movements of the stars brings knowledge of the visible universe.

Samyama on the navel brings knowledge of the growth and formation of the body.

Samyama on the appetites brings indifference to hunger, thirst and fatigue.

Samyama on the spine brings the quality of stillness.

Samyama on the aura produces the ability to see beings of other dimensions.

Sutras 34–41

Attainment of miraculous powers is gained by long dedication to the work, even through many incarnations. But as a result of long past efforts they may appear spontaneously, as psychic extensions of the senses.

The yogi does not regard these powers as ends in themselves. Dwelling on them becomes an obstacle to higher samadhi.

Concentration of pranic energy via the nervous system enables the yogi to penetrate the body or mind of another, to levitate and clothe himself with light.

The yogi can die at will.

Sutras 42–47

Samyama on the reception of sounds produces clairaudience.

Samyama on the law of gravity gives control of the law.

Samyama on the universal mind gives access to all knowledge.

Samyama on the rates of vibration of matter on the physical and higher planes gives control of the vibrations. When this control is applied to his own body the yogi retains youthful vigour into old age.

Sutras 48–56

Samyama on the senses, on their powers, on the media in

which they work, and on the experience they provide, gives control of the senses. With control of the senses comes the ability to use them beyond the physical body.

But even these powers must be renounced. Otherwise at the very pinnacle of attainment, the yogi will be defeated by pride.

Samyama on the eternal now brings knowledge that all is transitory.

Freed from ignorance and yearnings, aware of totality, adepthood is reached.

PART 4   ILLUMINATION

Sutras 1–14
Extra-sensory ability may be inherited genetically. It may also be carried over from a previous incarnation. It can be developed by drugs, by mantras, by austerities or by concentration.

Evolution of species proceeds by perfecting the true nature built into every species, including man.

Sense of 'I am' creates mind. Furthermore it can create a series of minds. But the Atman watches over all of them.

Only he who is cleansed by the experience of samadhi is free from latent karma.

Latent karma becomes manifested only when conditions are opportune.

Karma is continuous. The chain of cause and effect is unbroken through changes of space and time, even through evolutionary change to a higher species.

Karma remains as long as the need for experience remains.

Sutras 15–24
Subconscious tendencies depend on cause and effect. They are stimulated by physical objects. Within physical objects are past and future, while the gunas are ceaselessly at work, unifying the whole.

The moods of the mind vary. As a result what is experienced also varies.

But the Atman remains steadfast.

The mind is a mirror midway between the external world and the Atman.
The Atman is that whereby the mind understands.
The mind is the instrument of the Atman.
The yogi does not confuse mind with Atman.

Sutras 25–34
The mind must practise unrelenting discrimination. Otherwise distractions born of old perceptions may arise.
Distractions are banished by persistent meditation. He who remains undistracted, even in the dazzling possession of psychic powers, achieves full samadhi.
He is freed from ignorance, from suffering and from karma.
Physical creation manifests to serve evolution of spirit. It is nothing compared to the universe of spirit.
He who gains knowledge of the universe of spirit is freed from all obstructions and impurities. The constant interaction of the gunas ceases in the psyche of such an enlightened one. Their work is accomplished.
The gunas are absorbed into matter.
The Atman emerges untainted as primal spirit.
The aspirant, now adept, is united with the whole.

These are the Yoga Sutras of Patanjali, as popular today in Europe and America as ever they were in India. In the next chapter Patanjali's system will be examined alongside its close relation Samkhya, and compared with the other four of the famous Six Systems of Indian philosophy.

CHAPTER 7
Yoga as Philosophy: The Six Systems

After Patanjali had systematized yoga, or to be more precise, raja yoga, in his justly celebrated Sutras the subject became understandable in an intellectual way. Previously it had merely been looked on as a system of self-development, an ascetic discipline which shunned all intellectual argument and maintained that the stage of moksa, liberation, which it sought, was beyond mind and therefore beyond philosophy. This is still the view of true yogis. In keeping with the Sramanic tradition the ultimate depository of the yoga system is to be found in the personal lives and examples of its devotees. No amount of discussion or formulation will get beyond that essential basis.

However, the academic world loves to categorize and so attempted to fit Patanjali's Sutras into the intellectual framework of Indian life. This was probably done against the wishes of practising yogis. There are no records to tell us one way or the other. It fitted yoga into this intellectual strait-jacket by coupling it with its illustrious contemporary, samkhya. The aims of yoga and samkhya are the same. The methods of achieving those aims are not in conflict. They are complementary in that yoga is primarily practical, while samkhya is essentially intellectual. Moreover samkhya possessed a more attractive cosmology and psychology, which yoga is able to subscribe to wholeheartedly.

Thus yoga became a subject of study in the universities of India along with other philosophies, and about the year AD 200 it was fitted into the scheme of the Six Systems of Philosophy, a position held to this day, although largely irrelevant to the true life and purpose of yoga – unlike the other five which sit fairly comfortably in the academic mould.

These Six Systems are not really complete in themselves, but are complementary to each other, so are looked on as six parts of a complete Indian system. The six grew out of sixty-two systems. They provide a metaphysics, a religion, an explanation of ultimate reality, and a means of salvation. They tend to be bracketed together in pairs. The oldest are Yoga and Samkhya, the next being Vaisesika and Nyaya, and the final pair Purva Mimamsa and Vedanta. They are often referred to as darsanas or points of view.

The founders of these systems are considered to be Patanjali of Yoga, Kapila of Samkhya, Gautama of Vaisesika, Kanada of Nyaya, Jaimini of Purva Mimamsa and Vyasa of Vedanta. Each of them propounded their systems in the form of short sutras whose elucidation requires lengthy commentaries. All seem to stand at the end of a long period of discussion and disputation (or practice in the case of yoga), rather than as initiators of anything new. The six were formulated from the previous sixty-two about the year AD 200 and take us right up to the present time as far as Indian philosophical speculation is concerned.

Vaisesika and Nyaya may be classified shortly as systems of cosmology and logic respectively. Both are atheistic and correspond to some extent to philosophy as traditionally taught in the universities of Europe and the Western world. The founder of Vaisesika was Kanada – sometimes also known as Kanabhaksa or Kanabhuj. He is dated somewhere around AD 200. The main work is known as Vaisesika Sutra. Vaisesika means that which explains the characteristics and differences between individual things. It has been called a theory of particulars.

It comprises a sixfold classification of objects which can be thought about and named. These are:

1   substance (dravya) comprising earth, air, fire, water, ether, time, space, soul and mind;
2   quality (guna) comprising colour, taste, smell, touch, heat, number, extension, individuality, connection, separation, priority, posteriority, knowledge, joy, pain, desire, aversion and will;
3   movement and activity (karma);

4   generality (samanya);
5   particularity (visesa);
6   inherence (samavaya).

A seventh was added later. This was non-existence, a concept which may well have been introduced under Buddhist influence.

Considering these categories it will be seen that the first three possess real objective existence. The other three are products of intellectual discrimination. The seventh of course has neither characteristic. Vaisesika is an atomistic doctrine. What we experience is made up of parts, and is non-eternal, but the ultimate component-atoms are external. The atoms connected with earth, air, light and water produce the four senses of touch, smell, sight and taste. Earth atoms may produce new qualities. This is not so likely with the other three. There can never be annihilation of everything. Atoms will always remain indestructible. Individuality is formed by perceptible souls, and certain atoms.

The atoms become visible only when they are combined. At certain times during the cosmogenic cycles – days and nights of Brahm – they are not combined. At such times nothing is visible and nothing appears to exist. During these nights of Brahm the individual souls continue to exist, just as do the individual atoms. These nights are necessary because the continual wanderings of the soul tire them, and they need to sleep. When they are fully refreshed a new cycle of creation begins because the souls reunite with certain atoms. The world again becomes manifest. The particular atom with which the soul combined was the organ of thought.

Nyaya is attributed to Gautama who, it is said, lived about 150 BC. Another name for Gautama, really a nickname, is Aksapada, meaning one with his eyes fixed on his feet. This nickname may have been due to his considerable ability in logic, with all the hair-splitting analysis that the science requires.

His system treats of logic, induction, causation, comparison and metaphysics. It also includes a theory of knowledge which is acquired by intuition, inference, comparison and verbal testimony. It parallels Vaisesika in its atomism, cosmology and psychology.

The source book is Nyaya-Sutra, which is divided into five sections. The first defines the categories to be discussed in the later sections. The second deals with doubt, the four means of proof and their validity, and demonstrates that there is no other way. The third section considers the nature of man: ego, body, senses, cognition and mind. The fourth section considers reincarnation and karma, pain, volition, faults and failings, and enlightenment. This section also enlarges on a theory of error, and of the whole and its parts. The final section deals with unreal objections (jati) and situations calling for rebuke of an opponent (nigrahasthana).

The Nyaya-Sutra recognizes four sources of knowledge; perception (pratyahara), inference (anumana), analogy (upamana) and credible testimony (sabda). Logical discussion of a proposition takes the form of a syllogism which is in five parts. These are:

1   the proposition (pratijna),
2   the cause (hetu),
3   the exemplification (drstanta),
4   the recapitulation (upanaya),
5   the conclusion (nigamana).

The two systems, Vaisesika and Nyaya, were combined by Kusumanjali of Udayana round about AD 900 in his proof of the existence of God. From his time the two systems have been theistic. Although these two systems seem very different from Patanjali's Yoga and Kapila's Samkhya, Gautama in the fourth section of his sutra asserts that liberation can ultimately be achieved by ascetic detachment on reaching the highest stages of samadhi. It is interesting that the Jains claim early parentage for the Vaisesika system in their text known as the Avasyakna. As with so much else in Indian thought, it is more than likely that both Kanada and Gautama were formulating a tradition already ancient rather than anything new.

Purva Mimamsa and Vedanta are bracketed together as clarifying the teachings of the Vedas. Early writers in the

Mimamsa school were atheistic, later writers were theistic. The school set out to define Vedic liturgy, or the priestly duties in a logical form, though it was not a system of logic in the Western sense. It considers the Vedas to be infallible. One important idea is the theory of self-evidence – Svatah Pramana. Truth is its own guarantee. Cognitions are valid, unless discrepancies can be proved. Repeated testings will lead to the correct result in the end. This, of course, is in line with Western scientific investigations.

The Mimamsa asserts that the world of appearances is real, and so are individual souls. It also propounds the principle of Apurva – the link between cause and effect. So every act produces its effect some time or other. This idea is linked specifically with Vedic ritual in asserting the value of any ritual act as having a good effect eventually.

An extremely valuable and powerful concept derived from this school is dharma. This may be translated as duty, but its meaning is spiritual rather than social duty. If the one conflicts with the other the spiritual duty has priority. It is duty to oneself primarily – 'to thine own self be true', as Shakespeare has it. Having regard to the fact that we carry a load of past karma with us into this life, our duty is to recognize this, to ascertain the nature of it, and to lessen or eliminate it by doing our spiritual duty. The opening scene of the Bhagavad Gita highlights the dilemma of one's dharma as Arjuna agonizes over what he must do on the battlefield of Kurukshetra.

We have said that Mimamsa considers the Vedas to be infallible. It goes further in asserting that Sanskrit, the language of the Vedas, is not a language in the usual sense, but an emanation of Being (sat) in sound (sabda). So every sound in the fifty letters of the Sanskrit alphabet has a cosmic significance. The intoning of these sounds as sacred mantras can produce magical effects and lead us to truth. The Mimamsa considers that the mantric sounds are the most powerful element in any ritual.

In working off past karma it automatically follows that our behaviour in this life will be good and right. It may not appear to be so to others, and even to our socially conventional selves the directions our conscience compels us to take may appear to be contradictory, and even destructive. Thus life is in a state of constant tension between our social and spiritual dharmas.

Vedanta sets out to systematize the teachings of the Upanishads, considering these to complete and form the essence of the earlier Vedas. It is entirely theistic. Sankara was its main exponent. He produced a very pure monism, which has never been better stated in any culture in the world. Vedanta's other main exponents were Ramanuja, who initiated the Bhakti movement which swept North India in the middle ages, and Madhva.

Ramanuja was a theist. But his God was not the God of Sankara's monistic abstractions. It was a God of religious faith, a personal God, with the warmth and understanding of a human being. We should not doubt his reality because we cannot see or know him. Faith that he exists and is there is sufficient. Ramanuja's thinking is entirely in line with that of Christianity in these matters.

Within this supreme Brahman individual souls and the matter of the universe are merely attributes of his whole being. They are parts of supreme Brahman who is the creator of universes, but he does not create anything new. What appears as new to us is merely a modification of the subtle which we cannot see to the gross which we can see. We commune with this God by prayer, devotion and faith.

Whereas Sankara follows the yoga tradition in gaining liberation by removing all sensory barriers in order to find and unite with the Brahman within, Ramanuja says we realize Brahman by devotion and faith. According to Ramanuja the individual is not effaced when the goal is won. He maintains his self-identity, and enjoys the fruits of his faith. This is very close to Christianity, and very far from Buddhism's anatta doctrine of the disappearance of the self on realizing nirvana.

Madhva followed Ramanuja as a leading exponent of Vedanta. He reinforced Ramanuja theism, but placed a greater emphasis on the individuality of souls and the persistence of this individuality through successive incarnations. His teaching is an unqualified dualism. He makes five great distinctions within this dualism: God and soul, God and matter, soul and matter, one soul and another, and part of matter and another.

Reality for Madhva is neither independent (svatantra) nor dependent (paratantra). God is independent. Souls and matter are dependent. God controls souls and matter, but does not create or destroy. God did not cause the universe. He is part of it and by his presence keeps it in motion. Madhva also asserted that though dependent on Brahman, individual souls are active agents with responsibilities. No two souls are alike. The soul pervades and controls the body because of intelligence. God pervades everything including souls and bodies.

We have said that yoga sits uncomfortably among the Six Systems of Philosophy. It is the odd man out because it is not an intellectual system which the others are, and which the West understands as philosophy. It is an experiential system, a method of personal practice. It is included in the Six only on the strength of Patanjali's Sutras.

Because it is non-intellectual and even anti-intellectual, yoga has never felt the need to have a carefully worked-out rational explanation for things. Any explanation only becomes apparent in the course of actual experience. For those who look for such a rational explanation it points to a system of thought almost as old as itself, and whose tenets accord very closely with its own. This is the Samkhya philosophy.

In the course of time the two have become almost identical as far as their thought is concerned. This applies only to India. Samkhya has been looked on as the theory and yoga as the practice of the same basic philosophy. Both agree on ends. The object of existence is to realize moksa, release or liberation. This means release from the obscurations caused by mind stuff and sense objects. Then we can see through the fog created by the mind, and by the senses we can experience our true Self in all its pristine purity. When this happens the world and all our activities appear as a picture show, having no permanent reality. Although we continue to live and act we are no longer involved in it as we were formerly. We are detached because we now understand it. So both samkhya and yoga agree that true understanding can only come with the experience of moksa.

Samkhya believes that matter and the universe are real and not an illusion of the mind. It also believes in an infinite number of individual souls which are not emanations from a single world soul. Within each gross material body is another, subtle body, which comprises the psychic nature and the individuality. It is the subtle body which is the basis of rebirth, as well as being the individuality which persists through the various lives.

Samkhya presents existence as comprising two basic elements. This are prakriti (matter), and purusha (spirit). Prakriti is the basis of the material universe, and is manifest in three ways, or three stages of development. These are the three gunas. They are tamas (solidity and inertia), rajas (activity and energy), and sattva (light and intellect).

Sattva is the highest manifestation, and the quality to be aimed at and realized. Tamas provide obstacles to this realization. Rajas is the force by which obstacles can be overcome. All matter is under the rulership of the three gunas.

Prakriti depends on purusha, but purusha is independent of everything. Purusha is conscious while prakriti is unconscious. Prakriti evolves under the influence of purusha so that the intelligent Self may enjoy experience. It does this by developing sense organs and consciousness.

The first stage in the evolution of prakriti as far as humanity is concerned is mahat (greatness) and buddhi (intelligence). Next comes ahamkara, (the sense of the self, or the ego). From all these arises manas (mind), the five senses and the five organs of action. These developments are in the quality of sattva. Lower down the scale – deeper into matter – are the five tanmatras (fine elements), and from these arise five gross elements.

Samkhya posits an infinite number of individual selves. If they were not individual, then when one realized moksa all would realize it. We attain moksa when we realize that we are purusha, and so distance ourselves from prakriti. The pure Self is beyond intellect. The reflection of Self in intellect appears as ego. The evolution of nature is adapted to the ends of the Self. When Self realizes its distinction from the world of evolution and dissolution the latter ceases to operate in it. Nature (prakriti) continues to evolve because individual selves in it do not realize that they are really purusha and therefore can separate themselves from it.

Samkhya also teaches that cause and effect are merely the undeveloped and developed states of the same process; a kind of dialectic in the Hegelian sense. It also teaches that there can never be complete annihilation of everything. There will always be prakriti in some form, with the gunas and purusha working through it.

Yoga has accepted all these ideas, and found them satisfactory in that they accord with what yogis have experienced in their individual efforts to attain moksa. There are however three points of difference. The first is that samkhya is atheistic whereas Patanjali's version of yoga is theistic. As Patanjali came at the end of a long and ancient line of yogis it is by no means certain that earlier yoga was not atheistic, or perhaps agnostic. It seems more likely that in view of its traditionally close connection with both samkhya and Jainism it was so. Agnosticism is really much closer to the spirit of yoga than either theism or atheism. Patanjali after all was a child of his time, and he may well have been influenced by the rising tide of theism and bhakti, which was to reach full flowering in the life of Ramanuja.

The second divergence is due to the yogic insistence on first-hand experience of the ideas propounded in samkhya. Thus samkhya puts forward a great many concepts and categories of thought, and appeals to tradition to support them. Yoga by contrast appeals only to first-hand experience to prove the validity of the same concepts and categories of thought.

The third divergence, which is quite minor, is that samkhya describes the inner world of disciplined mind in terms of the thirteen evolutes. These are buddhi, ahamkara, manas, and the ten indriyas. Patanjali subsumes all these under the single concept of citta. Citta means to think, and denotes whatever is experienced or enacted by mind. So it comprises observing, thinking and desiring or intending. Therefore it combines both the reasoning faculty and the heart. Normally heart and mind behave as one. Thought is directed and coloured by our emotional biases and trends. Severe discipline and concentration is required to separate them, as is often necessary in scientific investigation. The samkhya teaching is static and analytical, explaining the situation in terms of differences, whereas Patanjali's concept is essentially psychological, warm and dynamic.

Samkhya, like yoga and Jainism does not accept the authority of the Vedas. The other four of the Six Systems do, so the three remain outside the orthodox group, though their importance is such that orthodoxy does accept them. They continue the tradition of the pre-Vedic, pre-Aryan, Dravidian culture of India, making what we have referred to collectively as the Sramanic stream. There seems little doubt that they continue long after the Vedic schools of philosophy have passed. Indeed we can already discern a process of absorption, for example, the important dharma concept of the Mimamsa philosophy appeared in the Bhagavad Gita and is now taught as part of yoga by many authorities because it is complementary to so many of the yoga-samkhya ideas.

Vedanta too is also looked on as yogic by many authorities. It must be realized that the early Upanishads were not written by Brahmins, but by yogis and other heterodox munis and rishis who stood outside and indeed were excluded from the mainstream of Brahminism. When Brahminism adopted the Upanishads it became Vedanta. As we have said before, Vedanta means end of the Vedas. The Upanishads were tagged on to the end of the Vedas, so Vedanta is based on the Upanishads. The Vedas themselves are now largely ignored. So even the most orthodox of the Six Systems, the Vedanta, is founded on yoga writings and ideas. Sankara, the leading exponent of Vedanta, declared himself and was declared by others to be a yogi. He practised yoga, as do indeed many Vedantists today.

Vaisesika and Nyaya are as we have said systems of philosophy as understood in the Western sense. They are purely intellectual exercises having no psychological or emotional warmth. They are academic disciplines divorced from real life. As such they are ignored by yoga, and are steadily being supplanted in India by new ideas imported from the West. They are not exportable systems as the other four have proved to be.

If we look at the cultural life of India today it is evident that, though everybody pays lip-service to Vedanta and it is the religion of the educated minority, the life of the villages is based on the older Brahminism. The caste system is still strong, the priests are still powerful, and life revolves around the local temple. A high proportion of the people practise yoga, even though few of them read or listen to recitations of the Upanishads.

So, as always throughout history, India presents its usual untidy picture. The neat schema of the Six Systems looks less neat and tidy outside the pages of books, or outside the universities in which they are taught. Today altogether new systems of thought are in vogue, chief among them being Scientific Humanism and Marxism. Both are having a considerable influence on the young people of India, and will undoubtedly modify still further the orthodox views.

These newer philosophies, like those of the older Dravidian culture, are agnostic or atheistic. Yoga is practised by their devotees just as assiduously as by followers of the theistic Vedanta. Because practice is so paramount in yoga the question of whether there is a God or not is secondary. Although Patanjali asserted in his Sutras that there was a God the teaching remains irrelevant to the mainstream of yoga practice. Yoga still stands as a philosophy among the Six Systems, but has already broken out of that mould as it has spread throughout the world.

CHAPTER 8
Mahayana Buddhism

By the second century AD Buddhism in India was in decline. It had settled down to a rather lifeless repetition of the ideas enshrined in the Buddha's first sermon, with some later embellishments. Much of early Buddhism consists of commentaries on the four noble truths, the eightfold path, the three signs of being, and the ideas of avidya (ignorance) and anatta (no soul). The ethics were indistinguishable from the Brahminism surrounding it. The boddhisattvas (enlightened ones) became similar to the Hindu gods, and were worshipped in much the same way.

The literature had grown to enormous proportions. Much of it was preserved in the south Indian language, Pali, which was also the language of Burma and Sri Lanka. As the literature grew the essential yogic message of the Buddha became obscured. His message as we have seen was entirely yogic, insisting on the necessity of experience and self-effort.

Into this situation was born Nagarjuna. His dates are unknown, and he can only be placed as being born between AD 200 and 300. What is known of him is from his biography translated into Chinese by Kunarajiva about AD 405. The original version seems to have been lost. He was born of a Brahmin family in south India, and while still quite young travelled north to the Himalayas. There a rishi of great age is stated to have transmitted to him the Mahayana Sutra, following which Nagaraja, the serpent king, disclosed to him an authentic commentary on it. These sacred teachings had been preserved for centuries because mankind was not yet ready for the message they contained. They were stated to be the hidden teachings of Gotama himself. This is the legend.

Mankind had received centuries of preliminary training (Hinayana) in preparation for this higher teaching, which could now be put out to the world. Nagarjuna was the chosen intermediary and according to legend he taught for three hundred years. In spite of the legends about him he appears to have been a real person. His writings are revered in northern Buddhism second only to those of the Buddha himself.

The work named in the legend is the Prajna-paramita. Some parts of it are regarded by scholars as preceding Nagarjuna while others follow him. Whatever the origins there is no doubt that the Prajna-paramita changed the face of Buddhism: Nagarjuna saw further than his contemporaries into the power still latent in the teachings of Gotama. His version was metaphysical, and his way was the negative way so much beloved by mystics of all ages and cultures. It might be called the negative way to end all negative ways. It uses intellect to go beyond intellect into a negation of all concepts and all forms of language. The Buddha's teaching on living without support was here taken to its farthest point in eliminating even verbal and conceptual support.

The word yana means the whole of the Buddha's doctrine. Its literal meaning is vehicle or ferryboat. Nagarjuna named his version of the yana as Mahayana, or the great vehicle, and referred to the previous teachings as Hinayana, or the little vehicle. He chose these names to give force to his central doctrine or picture. This was the picture of the ferryboat carrying the devotees to the farther shore. The metaphor is much used in Buddhism, and was also used in Hinduism. The ferryboat was and still is of great importance to Indian life. It is usually the only means of crossing a river, a much more hazardous undertaking in a tropical country like India than in more temperate areas of the world. The river is the sea of samsara, and the other shore is nirvana, or enlightenment.

Among those sayings of the Buddha that are known as the middle length dialogues is a discourse on a raft. A man crosses a river on a raft. If he was so grateful to the raft for carrying him across that he carried the raft for the rest of his journey he would be a very foolish person indeed. In the same way the vehicle of the doctrine is to be left behind when those using it have crossed to the other shore. The rules of the earlier (Hinayana) doctrine are for beginners, not for the enlightened.

The metaphor is clear and simple thus far. But Nagarjuna then takes off into a more rarefied atmosphere of thought. When one is trying to reach the other shore everything is very real and urgent. But when the perfected man has reached it he looks back, and realizes that what he left behind has no real substance. It was a mirage and void. He realizes that ideas like enlightenment, ignorance, freedom and entanglements are preliminary helps, referring to no ultimate reality; they are mere hints or signposts for the traveller.

The paradoxical teaching of the Prajna-paramita is that the enlightened one realizes that no Buddha has ever come into existence to enlighten the world with Buddhist teachings. The most elementary error is to believe that nirvana is at all different from samsara. They are merely contrary attitudes of the semi-conscious individual towards himself and the world in which he lives. It is entirely subjective, with no outer correspondence.

Buddhist yoga, or at least the mental side of it, is designed to conduce to the understanding that there is no substantial ego. This is somewhat different from the older jnana yoga which implied that the ego was real, even though we might ultimately be prepared to merge it into the being of supreme Brahman. The Buddhist ascetic training and meditation is meant to prepare one for the realization that nothing ultimately has any substance. There are only spiritual processes, sensations, feelings and visions appearing and reappearing. They can be watched with complete detachment. They can also be set in motion or brought to rest. The suppression of desire, which is the greatest message of the earliest of Buddha's discourses, became meaningless when the detachment of this point of view has been attained.

This reading of reality, latent in earlier Indian thought, was taken to its extreme in Mahayana Buddhism. It is full of paradox and has provided material for much discussion in later Buddhist schools of philosophy. In all these discussions, however, allowance is always made for the aspirant's position along the road to enlightenment. So assertion and negation are always somewhat muted in the realization that it is all relative to our position along the route. All the concepts of Buddhism have this tentative quality. A word like void (sunyata), has meaning only for an ego which is clinging to the apparent reality of things. Even the most advanced concepts are not more than stepping stones. All the great volumes of initiatory conversations, questions, analyses and codifications merely screen the ultimate essence of the doctrine, which in the end is not a doctrine, it is an experience.

The Prajna-paramita is often translated as the Perfection of Transcendental Wisdom, or as The Wisdom of the Other Shore. Prajna means wisdom, paramita means the other shore which symbolizes the virtue for which the aspirant strives. The work is in form a series of dialogues conducted between a large circle of buddhas and boddhisattvas, with no humans present. In mocking conversation they entertain themselves with enigmatic statements about the unstatable, saying that there are no such things as Buddhism, enlightenment and nirvana, and setting verbal traps to catch each other out in showing the merest vestiges of belief in some aspects of reality. They try to avoid the dualism involved in implying that there is nirvana, because that implies samsara, and betrays their clinging to these concepts by however tenuous a hold. They carefully avoid referring to themselves for that betrays a lingering belief in individual existence. And so it goes on, a strange, bewildering and remarkably elevating document.

In the Vajracchedika, one of the most important documents of the Mahayana, we meet the following statement, which gives some indication of the tone and quality of this type of thought. 'Whosoever stands in the ferryboat going to the further shore shall bear in mind the rescue of all living beings, conducting them to release and extinction in the pure and perfect nirvana. And when by virtue of this attitude he has rescued all beings no being at all has been made to reach nirvana. Why so? Because if the saviour had the notion of the actual existence of any being he could not be called a perfectly enlightened one. If he had the conception of a being taking on a series of bodies in the process of reincarnation, or of an individual personality then he is not a boddhisattva. Why? Because there is no such thing as anything or anybody standing in the vehicle of the enlightened ones.'

In its paradoxical way Mahayana Buddhism is stating its

belief in the Buddhahood of all beings, unlike Hinayana which considered Buddhahood to be attainable only by a few. The earlier Hinayana emphasizes the treading of the path, observing the rules of the order and obeying the ethical disciplines. Mahayana considered all this to be irrelevant, even childish, and certainly not for those who have received some measure of enlightenment. For instead of helping them further such rules will be more likely to hold them back from the step into the unknown which they should now take.

Another quotation from the Vajracchedika will help to illustrate the nature of the next step in thought that the seeker after enlightenment must now take. 'The Buddha sets forth in the great ferryboat, but there is nothing from which he sets forth. He starts from the universe but really he starts from nowhere. The boat is manned with all the perfections, but is manned by no one. It finds its support in nothing whatsoever, and will find its support in the state of the all-knowing, which will serve it as a non-support. Moreover no one has set forth in the great ferryboat. No one will ever set forth in it, and no one is setting forth in it now. Why? Because neither the one setting forth, nor the goal for which he sets forth is to be found: therefore, who should be setting forth, and whither?'

Mahayana then is concerned more with those who have received some degree of enlightenment than those who have just began to tread the path, since they are adequately catered for by the Hinayana. The conceptions that make up the dharma (the doctrine) are without corresponding ultimate realities. They are part of the raft, to be cast aside when the journey has been accomplished.

The Buddhist yogi is taught, by means of the disciplines, to realize within such a peace as one realizes when looking into the realms of infinite space. He looks inwardly, and there experiences the wonders of his own nature. Through success-ive stages of self-control and meditation he realizes utter stillness and voidness unmodified by any thought and un-coloured by any emotion. In these deep meditative states he realizes that fundamentally nothing is happening to the true essence of his own nature, nothing to cause either distress or joy.

Nagarjuna was the founder of what later came to be known as the Madhyamika school of philosophy. It means the middle way. Later it divided into two factions, the Prasangikas and the Svatantrikas. The Prasangikas were radical metaphysicians, while the Svatantrikas were more moderate. The Madhyamika school concerned itself primarily with matters of nirvana, and generally speculated that it was the same experience as that of void (sunyata), which was neither existent nor non-existent.

This was the first of the Mahayana schools of philosophy. When Nagarjuna appeared on the scene there were two main Hinayana schools. These were the Sarvastavadins and the Vaibhasikas. The Sautantrikas were another important school. These schools occupied themselves with finding answers to several of the questions that the Buddha had failed to answer. One of these was why, if there is no permanent soul (anatta) can people reincarnate time and time again, and be the same people reincarnating? The Hinayana schools answered this by saying that the ego-process is a series of (santana) moments (ksana) of transient entities (dharmas). None of this is permanent. They follow each other in a chain of cause and effect. These casual chains appear to others – and indeed to ourselves – as real individuals. Unless we felt them to be real they would not survive. Yet really every phenomenal being is made up of a flux of particles that are entirely ephemeral. This is rather like the view of solid matter found by modern physics.

This Hinayana is taken further and says there is no thinker, only thoughts. The doctrine says that neither substance nor individual souls exist, but allows for the existence of certain infinitesimal units out of which the world illusion is compounded. Nirvana is simply the realization that the whole phenomenon is unreal.

The Sarvastavedins are considered to be realists. They set out seventy-five categories under which every thought and form of being can be subsumed. They are real with regard to their substance and exist in a series of births, durations and destructions. They come to an end when realization dawns and we enter into nirvana.

Another difficulty involved with the anatta doctrine is how

can suffering be experienced when there are no permanent egos to experience it. The Sautantrikas answer this by saying that our processes of thought do not give us a true picture of external reality, but follow each other in a thought series of their own. Interior thoughts about exterior things do not necessarily tell us the truth about them. Sufferings are thoughts created by previous thoughts and actions. The suffering ego is only the continuity of the series of suffering thought. A blind reflex is created from within, not caused from without.

The Vaibhasikas however dissent from this view by saying that the outer world is open to direct perception. For them there are two kinds of knowledge: inference and perception. Suffering is an actual impingement of the outer world on the inner state of mind, though the inference that an enduring individual is suffering the ordeal is without basis in fact.

These Hinayana schools consider that the aggregates of experience, both inner and outer, are real but ephemeral. Mahayana goes further along the road by declaring that none of it is real. All phenomena are without substance. The world and everything in it cannot be described in terms of phenomena. The Mahayana describes the mystery of it all as tathata (suchness). This suchness cannot be described in words. From one point of view it is nirvana, from the point of view of knowledge it is boddhi. This Mahayana view takes us very close to the Sankara view of Brahman-Atman, of which nothing can be said, but which can only be experienced.

Mahayana considered the reality and existences of the Hinayana doctrines by positing three aspects of the reality of an object. These are quintessence, attributes and activities. For example, the quintessence of a jar is clay, its attributes are its shape, while its activities are its functions as a receptacle. Attributes and activities can change but quintessence is indestructible. Thus individual human beings are born and die, but humanity the quintessence endures.

The only final truth is the void (sunyata), the state of being thus – tathata, which is opposed to the ever-changing flux of phenomena. This is the absolute which endures through time and space as the essence of things. The realm of reality is absolute truth (paramartha-tattva), not of relative truth (samvrit-tattva). The description is almost exactly that of Sankara's supreme Brahman.

In the Madhyamika Sastra (Guidebook of the School of the Middle Way) it is said of the void, the central teaching of the Mahayana, that, 'It cannot be called void or not void, or both or neither, but in order to indicate it we call it the void.' This negative way of putting virtually all his teaching gives Nagarjuna's writings their unique character. Much of it is not new, particularly to those already steeped in the Upanishadic and Vedantic teachings, but the continual use of paradox, and the steadfast refusal to grant the mind a foothold anywhere makes for poetry and gives all these teachings a quite haunting beauty.

Perhaps this has helped it to endure when more reasoned expositions have disappeared. Nagarjuna's lead has been followed, and the same style has been carried through with a bold consistency in every phase of thought and feeling. Here the yogic virtue of detachment is carried through to the very limit. Sunyata for Nagarjuna carries the fullest possible statement about reality, and it does this because it is not a concept but a pedagogic instrument for realization. As the Buddha is supposed to have said in the Prajna-paramita, 'O Subhuti, all dharmas have sunyata for their refuge; they do not alter their refuge.'

The Prajna-paramita, as we have said, is paradoxical throughout. In its one thousand shlekas (couplets) it unfolds the idea of a long line of Buddhas, of which Gotama was only the latest; an almost exact restatement of the Indian doctrine of avatars. It also forecasts the next Buddha, the Buddha Maitreya, and it postulates the idea of the Boddhisattva.

In the Prajna-paramita are found the famous Diamond Sutra and also the equally famous mantra 'OM Mani Padme Hum' (Hail the Jewel in the Lotus). It is not so much a work of intellect as a series of meditations. Only by meditation can its value be appreciated. Prajna is the chief of six paramitas or cardinal virtues and means boundless wisdom. The others are dana (boundless charity), shila (boundless morality), kshanti (boundless patience), virya (boundless industry) and dhyana (boundless meditation).

The Prajna-paramita ends as paradoxically, making a

dramatic and poetic statement which teaches nothing: 'The wisdom of the other shore is the great magic formula, the formula of great wisdom, capable of allaying every suffering. It is truth because it is not falsehood. The formula is as follows: "Oh you have not gone before, gone to the other shore, who have landed on the other shore. Oh what enlightenment! Hail." Here ends the manual of the wisdom of the other shore.'

The brothers Asanga and Vasabandu developed the Yoga-cara philosophy from the legacy left by Nagarjuna. Their birthdates are unknown, but were certainly between AD 300 and 400. They rationalized Nagarjuna's doctrine of the void. Nirvana, they said, was not the same thing as the void. It was positive, filled with consciousness. It was the nature of this consciousness that they set out to study.

In the process of their rationalizations yoga disciplines and practices were again brought to the forefront of Buddhist thought. Asanga and Vasabandu were first and second of three brothers. They were Brahmins of Gandhara, and took orders in the Sarvastavedin school of the Hinayana. Asanga was the first to declare allegiance to the Mahayana. Both brothers were associated with the Gupta court of Ayodhya, present day Oudh, and were contemporaries of King Baladitya.

Vasabandu is credited with over twenty works, of which the Abhidharmakasa, meaning Compendium of Supreme Truth, dating from his early Hinayana phase, and the Vij-naptimatrata-tramishka, meaning Treatise in thirty stanzas on the World as Mere Representation, belonging to his Mahayana phase, are the most important. Asanga's main works were Yogacaryabhumi, meaning Stages of Yogacara, and Mahayana Sanpanigraha, meaning Mahayana Manual.

Yogacara stands for experientialism and mentalism. Physical objects must be defined in terms of what is experienced, but what is experienced is not just sensations or mental events. Yogacara does not deny that there are things external to the observer, but disclaims their independent existence and objects to their being equated with mind. The void is identified with pure consciousness, pure thought, true wisdom, as in Vedanta, and a system of reasoning is developed from this point. How, it was asked, was the phenomenal world produced from void if pure thought creates the phantasms called things and beings, and if pure thought realizes their voidness, how does it do this?

Whatever is created, it says, is created from within, by imagination. This thought is only possible because there is an eternal repository from which can be drawn the substance of every possible image and idea. This is alaya-vijnana, repository consciousness, or thought without the thing thought about, thought that is void, tathata – suchness, the positive aspect of void. The alaya-vijnana is potentiality, and this pure consciousness can be realized by mental yoga. This alaya is also the repository of klesa, the bad, as well as of kusala, the good, the happy and the auspicious.

The Yogacara philosophy has been termed Nir-alambana-vada, the doctrine of no support, since it denies that any external objects exist apart from mental processes to give external support to the constructions of the mind. It is also known as Vijnanavada, or doctrine of ideation, since it regards mere mental representation as the sole existence. It insists on the logical primacy not of created things, but of pure thought, which is the creating thing. Thought is positive. The rest is only the result of thought. Thought is luminous, but is obscured by defilements.

Yogacara illustrates that Buddhist metaphysics do not represent any fundamental departure from the mainstream of Indian thought. The Buddha merely approached the idea of moksa from an original standpoint. When the yoga element in either system came to the surface, as it did in Yogacara, they became virtually indistinguishable from each other.

When the Chinese Buddhist pilgrim Fa Hsien visited India about AD 400 he reported that four Buddhist schools of philosophy were fully developed there. These were Vaibhasika and Sautantrika of the earlier Hinayana doctrine, and Madhyamika and Yogacara representing Mahayana thought. He took back to China texts of all four schools. Hsuan Tsang visited India from AD 629-40, and reported that Hinayana and Mahayana were still strongly opposed to each other, although they both enjoyed good relations with Hinduism.

The disputations of the schools of philosophy did not, fortunately, exhaust the sum total of Buddhism at that time. A further aspect enjoying considerable popular support was the boddhisattva ideal. In Hinayana a boddhisattva is one who has experienced nirvana and is at the point of consecration into buddhahood. In Mahayana the term denotes a supremely compassionate being, who has remained to render help and comfort to lesser mortals.

Out of the egolessness of perfect indifference and perfect compassion he does not experience samyah sambodhi, the supreme enlightenment, and then pass on to parinirvana, the final extinction, but stops at the brink and takes the boddhisattva vow:

1   to bring about the liberation of all sentient beings;
2   to destroy all passions in myself;
3   to realize, then teach others, the truth;
4   to set others on the path to buddhahood;

The boddhisattva is invoked in popular worship because he has an inexhaustible power to save. His help is available at all times, and comes in many forms. The boddhisattva develops tapas or psychic heat, and is thus free from the elements. He is fearless, courageous and omnipotent. Boddhisattvas are practising the 'Great Yoga' (mahayoga) when they have these four qualities:

1   Realization that everything is a manifestation of Spirit;
2   Realization that there is such a thing as growth, or duration;
3   Understanding that the nature of external objects is non-existence;
4   Understanding that this knowledge can only be realized within ourselves.

This fourfold yoga rescues the practitioner from the painful whirlpool of samsara.

The great popular boddhisattva hero is Avalokitesvara. He is the personification of the highest ideal of the boddhisattva career. The legends state that after innumerable spotless incarnations he was able to enter the surcease of nirvana when a great wail went up from the earth and all its creatures. He therefore resolved not to enter the parinirvana which was his due until all other beings had entered before him. He is still worshipped today.

The potential boddhisattva must be active, humble and self-effacing, doing virtuous acts, and is entirely free from self-aggrandizement and display. Only action can set us free, but egoless acts imply a faith in the unknown. He must view all persons as potential buddhas and therefore treat them with respect. He must also continually practise all the yogas starting with hatha and pranayama to purify the subtle body, and so up the scale, right up to mahayoga.

Many stories are told of the temptations to which the boddhisattva is subjected. As it is the mark of a boddhisattva that thought and action are indistinguishable he does not think before acting. Accordingly, many stories are told of boddhisattvas who give away possessions, children, kingdoms and the like apparently on impulse. This saintly indifference to the normal values of human society is baffling, and meant to be. Nothing must be refused because refusal would be an admission that he still considered himself as possessing an ego, and to be a boddhisattva means to be egoless. The will and struggles for self-mastery of the old ascetics of an earlier age are here transformed from ego to universal.

One of the paradoxical sayings in the Prajna-paramita is when the Boddhisattva Avalokitesvara contemplates the wisdom of the other shore and considers that there are five elements of existence, but immediately perceives that they are void in their very nature. 'Here', he says, 'form is emptiness, and that very emptiness is form. Emptiness is not different from form. Form is not different from emptiness. What is form is emptiness. What is emptiness is form.' The five elements of existence referred to are:

1   Rupa (form), earth, air, fire, water, and everything springing from them;
2   Vedana (sensations, sense-perceptions and feelings);
3   Sanja (self-conscious intellection);
4   Samskara (predispositions and inclinations);
5   Vijnana (consciousness, discrimination and knowledge).

Along with these elements of existence are the twelve con-
catenations of cause and effect. They are:

1 Ignorance;
2 Action;
3 Consciousness;
4 Name and form;
5 Senses;
6 Contact;
7 Sensation;
8 Craving;
9 Attachment;
10 Becoming;
11 Rebirth;
12 Old age and death.

Contained within the Prajna-paramita is the Diamond
Sutra, and in it is a discourse on gifts. 'The Boddhisattva does
not give gifts. A gift should not be given if he believes in
objects, in anything, in form, in the special qualities of sound,
smell, taste and touch. A gift should be given only in order
that he should not believe even in the idea of a cause, and
why? Because that Boddhisattva who gives a gift without
believing in anything, the measure of his stock of merit is not
easy to learn.'

The Mahayana doctrine of the three bodies of the Buddha
– the trikaya doctrine – approaches very closely to the Hindu
concept of Brahman/Atman, Ishvara (the creator) and
Avatara (the historical incarnation). The trikaya are:

1 Dharmakhaya (essence body), which is identical with
   the void, suchness (tathata), divine knowledge (prajna)
   and wisdom (bohdi);
2 Sambhogakhya (body of bliss) which is the essence made
   manifest in heaven or the Buddha fields, within the laws
   of causality;
3 Nirmanakhya (body of transformation) which is the
   essence made manifest on earth as an historical Buddha
   emanated or projected from the Sambhogkhya.

The Dharmakhya later became personified as the Adi-
Buddha (supreme Buddha) whose consort is Prajna-paramita.

The symbol of this is the tantric symbol of Siva/Shakti in sexual embrace.

This symbol, which is the same as the Tibetan Yab Yum and is found in the earliest Indian writings and architecture, emphasizes the power of compassion (karuna) which holds everything in manifestation. The Mahayana school of the 'Great Delight' (mahasukka) uses this symbolism very fully to emphasize that samsara and nirvana are the same. In sex one realizes a state akin to nirvana while participating in an act the most samsaric. It amounts to an affirmation of the phenomenal world against the earlier world-negating ascetics. This school is believed to have originated under King Indrabhuti of Uddiyana in the seventh or eight centuries. He wrote a work, Jnanasiddhi, in which this symbolism is elaborated.

The Buddhist, like the Vedanta teachings, end in a dualism. Whatever is asserted, its opposite then becomes apparent. The unity always evades thought. The void and suchness – sunyata and tathata – the supremely negative way of seeing things was the Mahayana contribution. The mind systematically deprives itself of all supports, leaving consciousness without cerebration alone in the void. The boddhisattva ideal was also contributed as the ethical application of these great negative concepts. All things, buddhas, arahats, dharmas are void, even unto nothingness.

CHAPTER 9
Tantrism

Tantrism was a popular movement with a very subtle philosophy of active emotion. It can be described philosophically as existential. Emotionally, it marked the return of the mother goddess into the religious life of India. Although Hinduism today is nominally Vedantic, its active religious life is tantric. The same can be said of Mahayana Buddhism.

The philosophy of tantrism developed out of the philosophy of the Yogacara school, particularly that sub-division of it known as Vajrayana. It arose in north-east India, where so much of Indian religious life has had its birth. Main centres of tantrism were at Uddiyana in Orissa, Kamakhya in Assam, Sirihatta also in Assam and Vajrayogini of Purnagir in east Bengal. Orissa was the main centre. The teachings spread along with Mahayana Buddhism, and so found their way into Tibet, Mongolia and China.

The development of the philosophy out of Yogacara came by way of the Mahasukhavada school. This school addressed itself to the nature of nirvana, and reached a conclusion which was almost exactly that of the early Upanishads. It stated that nirvana was characterized by sunyata (void), vijnana (consciousness) and mahasukha (bliss). The early Upanishadic classification which was of the equivalent state of samadhi was sat (being), chit (consciousness) and ananda (bliss).

This school eventually became Vajrayana, and on its basis all true tantric practices were formulated. Vajrayana means the way of firmness. This way of firmness illustrates both the methods and the ideals of tantra. It prescribes rites and grades of practice depending on the spiritual character of the devotee. Here reference is made to the three gunas. The rajasic will require a different sadhana (way of worship) from the tamasic, and he again from the sattvic. The types are known in tantra as vira (hero), pasu (dull witted) and divya (saintly).

The word sadhana means the tantric type of active and highly emotional worship which is suited to one's own nature. A sadhaka is the devotee who worships and lives in a tantric way. It is instructive to note that vira, the hero or rajasic person, is considered to be the ideal in tantra, rather than the divya or saintly person. The latter had hitherto always been held up as the ideal. The reason why the hero or rajasic person is held up as the ideal is paradoxical, and needs to be meditated on. The fact that he is courageous and active in contrast with the saint who is passive has much to do with the choice. The saint retires not just from the world, but from his own emotions. The hero actively immerses himself in both.

Although tantra received its philosophical basis from the Vajrayana school of Mahayana Buddhism, its history is much older and takes us back to the early Sramanic stream of Indian thought. In its active aspect it can be looked on as a modern development of very ancient magical and fertility rites. In these ancient systems the most basic of human functions were worshipped and placated. In the excavations at Mohenjo Daro and Harappa can be found traces of the worship of the male principle in the form of the lingam (phallus) and of the female principle in the form of the yoni (vulva). From these early practices developed the Siva-Shakti cult which is so prominent a feature of tantrism. These early tantric practices were suppressed by the Aryans, who brought their own religion based on priesthood, sacrifice and caste. Obviously there was no compromise possible with the indigenous naturalistic and free-thinking worship of the native population.

There is as yet no means of knowing whether the early yogis participated in tantric practices. Probably they did not, as the orientation has always been towards meditation and other inward-looking mental practices. Yet in their development of siddhis (psychic powers) they may well have used some of the techniques in order to arouse a state of ecstasy, often necessary to achieve the desired result. However, tantra techniques have always been systematic, having a philosophic basis. This distinguishes tantra from shamanism, which used similar techniques, but in a less controlled and more selfish way in order to gain pleasure, wealth or power. One meaning of tantra is treatise, so tantra is activity and philosophy, and the tantras are treatises about them. In the main, the tantric yoga practices and philosophy are concerned with purification, and a mature philosophy is a fundamental necessary to tantric initiation.

The first written tantras appeared in the fourth century AD when the Yogacaras and later Vajrayana were at their most influential. They describe the practices of mantra (sounds of power), yantra (geometrical designs drawn on the ground), mandala (geometrical symbolic pictures on a wall), visualizations of gods and goddesses representing manifestations of energies or natural principles, asanas (physical postures), mudras (gestures), various aids to meditation, and the processes of sadhana (worship). Some early tantras were Gukyasavaja, Manjushrimulakalpa and Hevajratantra. The Prajna-paramita is often claimed as an early tantra also, but this claim is not very realistic.

Early tantras were confined to the Indian states of Assam, Bengal, Bihar and Orissa. Indrabhuti, King of Orissa, was instrumental in introducing tantrism into Tibet. His adopted son Padmsambhave defeated the native shamanbons at magic and subsequently founded the Ningmapa (red hat) sect of lamaism. Tantrism became incorporated not only into Buddhism and Hinduism, but also into Jainism, and also influenced Islam via the Sufis. Ardent Tibetans collected tantra manuscripts in Sanskrit, Bengali, Oriya and Assamese and incorporated them into their own canon, about one-third of which is tantric.

Today the best known tantras are Tantra-kaumudi, Saktisanyama, Rudramayamala, Kaliku Kularnava, Tantratattva and Mahanirvana. The last two of these were translated by Arthur Avalon under the title of 'The Serpent Power'. Every tantra should theoretically discuss five things:

1 Creation of the Universe;
2 Destruction of the Universe;
3 Worship of Gods;
4 Attainment of Supernatural Powers;
5 Union with Ultimate Reality.

The early tantras are supposed to be teachings imparted by Shiva to his consort Shakti. They deal with magic, mysticism, science, religion, medicine, metaphysics, mantras, yantras, mandalas, and kundalini. The yogatantras are concerned mainly with meditation.

All the Hindu tantras were opposed to caste, sex discrimination and sati – the custom which required the widow to throw herself on the dead husband's funeral pyre at his cremation. They have oftened been referred to as the fifth Veda. The Hindu tantras are also looked on as natural successors to the Puranas, which today along with the four Vedas are irrelevant and virtually unreadable. Sankara, the great reviver of Vedanta, listed sixty-four tantras as circulating during his lifetime – AD 686 to 719. In Hinduism the tantras are considered to be the religious books of one of their sects, the Saktas, and to be based on the Bhakti movement which swept India in the first century AD. Tantrism is also stated to be the correct form of worship for the Kali-yuga, the age in which we are now living, generally considered to be a dark age of destructive forces. It is taught that mankind has passed through three cycles or yugas. The first was Satya-Yuga, which was a golden age of enlightenment, then the Treta-Yuga, next the Dvapara-Yuga, and so to the present time, the Kali-Yuga. In the Vishnu Purana it is said that the Kali-yuga will be an age, 'Where property confers rank, wealth is a virtue, passion binds husband and wife, falsehood is the source of success, sex the only enjoyment, and outer trappings are confused with inner religion.' On the very large time scales spoken of in the Puranas these four yugas are part of a greater time-scale in which, starting from an elevated standpoint of great spirituality, mankind is progressively immersed deeper and deeper into matter until at the present time mankind is at his most materialistic level. From this point forward the descent into matter will be followed by a progressive ascent. Mankind will again attain the spiritual heights, but having incorporated into his essential nature all the vast experience of matter through which he has passed.

Tantra broke away from the main trends of the Vedas and of the Vedanta which followed, and also from the popular Hinduism of the epics and the Bhagavad Gita. It was open to

recognize caste. The yoga element again came to the surface.
Its practice was intensified and widened, and various sub-
divisions were established. These sub-divisions provided yet
again a graded system whereby the devotee could reach
enlightenment. The extended yoga that developed in tantra
included hatha yoga, a system of self-improvement that
became something more than just a series of postures, and
also laya or kundalini yoga. In what has come to be known as
tantric yoga proper the male/female polarity is accepted as a
way to enhanced ecstasy and joy, an acceptable path to
nirvana. Another thing that became more prominent in yoga
at that time was the importance of the guru or teacher.

The dualism that was central to samkhya and yoga was fully
accepted in tantra, with no effort being made to attempt a
synthesis. Tantra makes use of the underlying dualism of the
phenomenal world as a basis for actively and consciously
comprehending reality. All the energies and elements of the
phenomenal world are at the disposal of the yogi, even sexual
energy. The cosmic unity of the opposites can be said to be
the main activity of the tantra. It takes the whole psycho-
somatic constitution of the practitioner as a basis for realization, not just the mind as in intellection, or the spirit as in
mystical vision, or just the emotions as in bhakti. Some of the
complementary pairs of opposites in the tantric scheme have
been given as:

    aham (subject) – idam (object)
    sunyata (void) – karuna (compassion)
    prajna (wisdom) – upaya (means)
    prakriti (matter) – purusha (spirit)
    jivatman (individual soul) – paramatman (universal soul)
    samsara (phenomenon) – nirvana (enlightenment)
    shakti (energy) – shiva (consciousness)
    yum (mother) – yab (father)
    svarupa (form) – arupa (formless)
    yoni (female) – lingam (male)

One of tantra's most active, indeed ecstatic, aspects is the
worship of an ideal of some kind. This may be one of the
Hindu divinities. In Buddhism it is often a boddhisattva, principally Avalokitesvara. It can be the devotee's guru, living or

dead. It may also be an idealized women in the case of a man, and of a man in the case of a woman. Fascination and ecstasy are encouraged as a means to heighten emotion, and thus to the generation of greater power in realizing one's goal. It is said in the popular tantras that the gods relied on their shaktis or female consorts to enhance their powers. The female generates the energy. The same process goes for everybody. By intense love and worship of the consort – husband, wife or lover – one's own potentiality is enhanced. The physical union of lovers is a foretaste of the mystical union of realization in samadhi in Hinduism, or of nirvana in Buddhism. The ideal is to unite the male and female elements in ourselves, so the male meditates on female characteristics and vice versa. In this way the tantric yogi transcends sex, knowing both sides of the polarity. The worship of the beloved, be it male, female, guru, god or some divinity can be extremely elaborate. Ritualism and rich symbolism are encouraged. Many of these rites and rituals are described in the tantras. The object is to concentrate the mind and heighten the emotions to a state of ecstasy. In this way we make an approach to the bliss of nirvana.

In performing a tantric rite the bhuttashuddhi or cleansing process is an essential preliminary. It is done by active meditation on the seven main chakras, imagining each in turn being energized and cleansed. The sadhaka will bathe, dress and purify his thoughts. The object of worship, divinity, guru, lover etc., is welcomed as a guest with flowers, obeisance, washing of feet, jewels, perfume, incense, offerings, praise and conversation. The sadhaka will pray to the beloved, and describe the qualities of the beloved in appropriate terms. All the time he is aware that obliquely he is worshipping his own Self. The identity of the worshipper with the worshipped is the first principle of tantric devotion or sadhana.

Bhuttashuddhi is the process of raising kundalini. Thus the sadhaka imagines the kundalini force rising through the chakras, from the base of the spine to the top of the head. It is said that the vira (rajasic person) and the pasu (tamasic person) can imagine the kundalini as rising and cleansing the chakras, but in the case of the divya (sattvic person) it really does rise. Kundalini is roused if the devotee feels restless for the spiritual life.

In Indian tantrism theism takes the form of a personal god in the Christian sense. The important difference is that this personification is usually female. The mother goddess of the old fertility cults has certainly returned in tantrism. She is known under many names: Devi, Durga, Kali, Parvati, Uma, Sat, Padma, Candi, and Tripura-Sundari. After being eclipsed for a thousand years by the male deities of the Aryan Vedic pantheon, the goddess has been re-enthroned. Popular worship in India is now almost entirely tantric. This reinstatement of the goddess as the central figure in popular worship is yet another indication of the resurgence of the pre-Aryan, Dravidian and Sramanic stream of religious life. However, Indian tantrism still accepts the authority of the Vedas.

Tantra teaches that artha (prosperity), kama (fulfilment of sensual desires), dharma (spiritual and moral duty) and moksa (release from it all) are one. By virtue of his love for the goddess the devotee discovers that the fruit of these four falls into his hand. Tantrism insists on the holiness and purity of all things, hence the 'five forbidden things'. The ritual of the five forbidden things is distinctively tantric, and has given rise to misgivings and a great deal of misunderstanding. The five forbidden things are: grain, fish, wine, meat and sex. They are five good things for the vira, they are forbidden things for the pasu, and for the divya they are symbolic of other things: wine (madya) is intoxicating knowledge, meat (mamsa) is the act of assigning everything to God, fish (matsya) is empathy, grain (mudra) is the act of dissociating from all forms of evil, while sex (maithuna) is union of the highest and the lowest. This ritual is undertaken under the guidance of a guru. It is tantra of the left-hand path. The tantric hero (vira) goes through the sphere of greatest danger, and rises by means of nature, not by rejecting it. The creature of passion has only to wash away his sense of ego and the acts that were formerly an obstruction become the means of liberation. The tantra of the left-hand path takes us beyond asceticism and morality. Here wine, meat and sex are freely enjoyed. The object is to heighten mystical feeling. Another is to demonstrate that one can enjoy total freedom yet still be spiritual, more so in fact, because one has risen above the need to observe rules and ordinances, which really belong to spiritual childhood. Hindu tantra distinguishes between right-hand (dakshina), and left-hand (vama) sadhana, according to whether the contact with the five forbidden things is actual or symbolic. It will be realized that on compassionate grounds in largely vegetarian India both fish and meat are not eaten and that the word grain probably means some sort of drug.

There are four categories of tantric practice. The first is kriya tantra. This emphasizes man's behaviour as it expresses itself in deeds, thoughts and words. It calls for rigorous discipline of diet, celibacy, worship and meditation. The second is carya-tantra. This emphasizes man's behaviour as exemplary, rather than imitative. Whereas in kriya-tantra one feels subservient to the divine powers, in carya-tantra one is a friend of the divine powers. This is exemplified by the vira's taking the five forbidden things. The third is yoga-tantra. In this one seeks to transcend the separateness of oneself and the divine powers, struggling for unity with the divine. The desired state of concentration and integration is induced and stabilized by the 'five intuitions'. Yoga-tantra employs inner discipline, particularly watching the mind, and also visualization exercises. An important feature is guru initiation. Ritual purity is a feature of these first three tantras. The fourth category of tantric practice is anuttara-yoga-tantra. Here the practice goes to the utmost limit. Siddhis (psychic powers) are developed, and the sadhaka reaches to the void, realizing that everything is void in its essential nature.

The four categories of tantra practice are Buddhist. Hinduism followed suit somewhat later, the stages being very similar but with an essentially Hindu flavour. The four categories of Hindu tantric practice are vedachari, dakshina-chari, vamaschari and sidhantachari. Hindu tantra became mixed with Kapalika, Aghori, Nathist, Shaivite and Shakta rites, and with more primitive tribal and animistic influences, often involving sacrifice. In time, owing to these influences, it became very debased.

Tantra flourished on a grand scale in north-east India until the thirteenth century when Moslem invaders laid waste universities and other centres of learning, slaughtering inhabitants and burning books. This ended the golden age of tantra in India. However, it has continued to flourish in Tibet, Nepal and the Himalayas even to this day. It has revived in India, and is particularly strong in Bengal. In Tibet it was adopted by the priests of the Bon religion. The Bauls, a little known sect, still maintain the oral tradition. Bengal has produced many tantric gurus, including in the early period Shabaripa and Darikapada, in medieval times Sri Chaitanya, Krishnananda and Agamavigisa, and in the nineteenth century Paramahamsa Ramakrishna, Bamekepha and Sri Aurobindo. Tantra is at present enjoying a considerable vogue in the West.

Sadhana, as we have said is the practice of tantra. We have also said that tantra is systematic. This systematization shows up in its sub-division. Sadhana is undertaken in three phases. These are the starting point or foundation, the path or method, and the goal which is realization. The foundation assumes knowledge and practice of hatha yoga and pran-ayama, and of the yamas and niyamas. Usually there is also prior initiation by a guru. The path or method uses twelve practices. These are asanas, pranayama, pratyahara (sense withdrawal), mantrayana (words, syllables and sound), yantra, mudra (symbolic gestures), mandala, dhyana (meditation), sandhya (kundalini meditation), torpana (purification of the five elements), nyasa (identification in thought with parts of the body), and shuddhi (the rite of the five forbidden things). Among other numbered items can be mentioned the five agamas or tantric writings. These depend on the personifica-tion celebrated. In Hindu tantra they are Surya the Sun-God, Ganesh the elephantheaded son of Shiva, Sakti, Shiva and Vishnu. Tantra continually returns the sadhaka to the four fundamental questions: Who am I? Where have I come from? Where am I going to? Why am I here?, and calls for regular repetition of the formula: 'The whole of existence arises in me, the three-fold world. I am pervaded by it all. The world consists only of this.'

Tantra can be said to be all about aesthetic experience. As aesthetics it cannot be formalized in any way. It has been described as a weave, with various strands of warp and weft making a complex and pleasing pattern. The Tibetan master Klong-chen rab-byams-pa has stated, 'Tantra as actuality means starting point, path and goal. It is a trinity of nothingness, translucency and aesthetic awareness. It makes experience and judgment possible and ever present as the origin of samsara, and of nirvana. Tantra is continuity. It is existential and immediate.'

The point that tantric yoga makes is that tantra is not something separate in relation to the being of man. Tantra is coterminous with man's being, a process, like life itself. There can be no limit to the diversity of its aspects. It is concerned with awareness, which is the beginning of mental activity, and with the distinctive colour or warmth or emotion we feel as awareness dawns. The aesthetic awareness and experience continues through all stages of enlightenment up to samadhi or nirvana, at which point the mental constructs we have added en route are swept away. We then return to the basic aesthetic awareness experience, but purified of the dross of concepts, words and rules. Existentially tantra is the essential individual nature of man as a constant possibility, not something reducible to an entity defined by rational concepts. It is grounded in man's freedom.

The wealth of psychological information contained in the tantras does not constitute a science of psychology. Tantric, like traditional, yoga is not concerned to be scientific. It addresses itself to man's uniqueness as a living being, and not to any theoretical schema. The tantras are not accessible to traditional methods of rationalization. They deal with life as it is lived, and as life can be lived. In all this relativity there is the problem of gaining a foothold for thought. Cutting the Gordian knot, tantra overcomes the problem by boldly asserting that the ground of our being is emotional, and female. It puts forward the symbol of the mother goddess as a verbal symbol for nothing, not an empty nothing but a nothing of power. When we have become aware of this dynamic nothing it resides as an aesthetic experience in the present moment.

Tantra recognizes the female principle as providing inspiration, friendliness, tenderness and intimacy. It arouses emotions of the right kind. The union of two lovers is one of the most powerful of these. By accepting the centrality of emotion tantra teaches the art of living. The sadhaka is interested in fathoming life. He embraces maya and does not reject it. He aims at the state of prema – ecstatic, egoless, beatific bliss in realization of transcendent identity. The tantric formula is that yoga (discipline), and bhoga (enjoyment) can be and are the same, but it takes a vira (hero) to confront and assimilate both. Tantra dispels illusion.

CHAPTER 10
Vedanta

Vedanta represents an attempt by a reformed Hinduism to recover ground lost to Tantrism and Buddhism. Most educated Hindus would today consider themselves to be Vedantist, and more specifically of that form known as Adviata, the form bequeathed to posterity by Sankaracharaya. Adviata means non-dualism, so Sankara – the acharaya suffix means great teacher – stands in that long tradition of Indian thinkers who have attempted to get beyond the dualism inseparable from phenomena to the essential unity behind all manifestation. With Sankara the Sranamic ideal again prevailed, even though he is now considered to be entirely orthodox. The Sranamics did not accept a supreme godhead to which the individual soul was subservient. To them the aim was to retain their individual identity throughout time, and to realize their essential isolation (kaivalya). In advaita the Sranamic ideal prevailed as Atman-Brahman, the unified godhead that is aloof from the world of purusha and prakriti, and the workings of the three gunas.

Sankara fully embraced the early Upanishads, and based his reasoning on the formula first met with in the Chandogya Upanishad, 'Tat Tvam Asi', 'You Are It, i.e. Atman and Brahman are one and the same. The fundamental thought of Advaita is that the embodied soul (jiva) is the Self (Atman), which when we see through the mists of maya is Brahman. At the same time Advaita accepts the authority of the Vedas. The candidate for Vedanta must fulfil the normal religious duties, be qualified by birth, have studied the four Vedas, and be able by the practice of yoga to be able to discriminate between the permanent and the transient, and to have a guru.

Sankara wrote commentaries on the Brahmasutra, the Bhagavad Gita and the Upanishads. His principal work is the Viveka Chudamani, The Crest Jewel of Discrimination. He was born at Kaladi in south India. Born in AD 686, he died in AD 719 at the age of thirty-three (the same age as Jesus Christ), so for the whole of his short life he was youthful, vigorous and idealistic. He set out to purify Hinduism by advocating an extreme asceticism, and by teaching a pure monism based on the Atman-Brahman equation. In the process of turning Hinduism back to its fountainhead he was also responsible for driving out Buddhism which by then had lost all direction, and been subverted by a variety of compromises with the lower and more popular forms of Hinduism. The emperor Ashoka had more or less foisted Buddhism on the peoples of India, so its hold had always been somewhat tenuous. The Indian mind, though highly syncretistic, needs a long time to assimilate new ideas. Buddhism was not going to be taken up that easily.

Sankara was a Brahmin, which gave him a head start. He would not have been listened to if he had not been a Brahmin. From all accounts he was evidently a very happy and relaxed person, whose company people enjoyed. Perhaps Krishna was his model quite apart from his own innate charm. Legendary accounts of Krishna dwell on his beauty and intelligence, and Sankara had these in abundance. At the age of ten he was disputing with learned men in the temples, exactly like Jesus before him. Shortly afterwards he took the monastic vows of poverty and chastity, and began his life's work.

He met the man who was to be his guru, Govindapada, who taught him many yoga principles and the raja yoga techniques of concentration and meditation. Spontaneously Sankara took to them, and equally spontaneously achieved samadhi. From this point forward there was nothing more that Govindapada could teach him. Sankara went joyously on his way, transmitting his teachings as he went. He lectured continuously and wrote copiously. He wrote poems, hymns and commentaries. His commentaries on the principal Upanishads and the Bhagavad Gita are read to this day. As well as the Viveka Chudamani, he wrote the Upadeshasahasri, and also left behind him many tracts, aphorisms and prayers.

In addition to his teaching he was an energetic organizer, following the example of Buddhism by establishing many monasteries and ten monastic orders. Many still survive, though India for some reason does not take kindly to monasticism.

The Viveka Chudamani, The Crest Jewel of Discrimination, is the clearest and most comprehensive statement of Sankara's philosophy. Written in a direct style, in verse, it is quite different from his commentaries, which kept within the didactic style cultivated by scholars in his day. It is summarized here by taking out some of the more telling passages, and those that are more relevant to our times. His references to Brahmins, to women and to caste for example would not endear him to most modern readers. It opens with a salutation to Govinda, his own guru, one who has attained the bliss of samadhi, and begins:

'It is difficult to attain birth in a human body. To be born pure, and with a desire for learning and spiritual attainment comes only after thousands of incarnations. To meet with an advanced spiritual teacher, this also is difficult, but will happen if your previous development has prepared you for it.

Strive to find a genuine spiritual teacher, a guru, and by practice of yoga learn discrimination. Study the ancient spiritual writings, and by tranquility and purification try to gain knowledge of the Atman.

You must be intelligent, learned and resolute to attain success in this task. You must also cultivate detachment, be tranquil and eschew enjoyment.

You must be without desire, be humble, and be devoted to your task of seeking liberation from the things of this world.

To attain to liberation there are four preliminary steps. The first is to learn to discriminate between the eternal and the transitory. The second is to renounce the enjoyment of the results of your actions. The third is to renounce all possessions. The fourth is earnestly to aspire to liberation. You must learn to concentrate the mind on an object and keep it from wandering. You must also learn to confine the senses to their proper sphere, and not let them wander. You must endure pain and sorrow without complaint, and must meditate on the ancient writings, or on the words of the guru, without ceasing. But among the means to be used in our search for liberation the foremost is devotion.

The earnest seeker after liberation must approach a learned man of spiritual attainment, one who has already attained to liberation, and seek his help in the quest. The student says, "Great soul, I have again returned to the round of death and rebirth. What must I do to be liberated from it?"

The master replies, "Have no fear. There is a means to cross the ocean of worldliness, and reach the other shore. This is the means by which the yogis have crossed. The ancient writings have said that sraddha (learning), bhakti (love), dhyana (meditation) and yoga (self discipline) will bring the results you require. These will release you from the bondage of reincarnation."

The student asks, "What is this bondage? How did it begin? Why does it continue? What is spirit? What is not spirit? How can I distinguish between them?"

The master replies, "Your questions again delight me. You are already well advanced along the road. But realize that you must make the effort of emancipation yourself. If you are hungry you can only assuage it by taking food yourself. If you are sick you can only cure it by taking medicine yourself. The nature of reality can only be seen yourself, not by following the vision of another. The bonds of past karma can only be loosed by yourself.

One cannot be liberated by philosophical speculation, by much learning or by developing extraordinary powers. These are merely distractions. The chief means for liberation is detachment of the mind from all such distractions.

I will now tell you the distinction between spirit and non-spirit, which is the question you asked. The physical body comprises many substances, made from the five elements of earth, air, fire, water and ether. It also comprises separate parts, and five sense organs. This physical body is the root cause of delusion.

Sensuous objects are more deadly than the poison of the cobra. Only the person who is free from desire, so difficult to renounce, is ready for liberation. Even the very learned, those skilled in the Six Systems of Philosophy, even they cannot attain it if full of the sense of enjoyment.

Turn away from enjoyment of the sense, and instead enjoy peace, contentment, tranquility, forgiveness and self-control.

Free yourself from all attachments to home, husband, wife, children and friends. Above all free yourself from attachment to the body.

The physical body is born as a result of the karma of previous lives. It is subject to birth, decay and death. It is subject to changes as it moves from birth to death. It has organs of perception and action, and the mental powers of mind, intellect, ego and emotion. Mind considers different aspects of an object. Intellect tries to fathom its true nature. Ego is the sense of self, of I and mine. Emotion reacts to whatever pleases or threatens us.

The subtle or astral body is the seat of our desires. Within it the results of past karma are experienced. It is closely associated with the Atman. The dream state belongs to it. The subtle body is the tool of the Atman. Yet the Atman is not tainted by it.

The mind identifies with perception, and with the activity of the physical body. That which believes itself to be initiating action and experience is the ego. The ego acts under the influence of the three gunas, and experiences the three states of consciousness, waking, dreaming, and dreamless sleep.

The individual may experience pain, but the Atman experiences bliss at all times. If you love an object you love it not for itself, but for the love of the Atman. Realize this. In dreamless sleep there is no object to experience. So in this state the blissful state of the Atman may be inferred.

Maya gave birth to this universe. Maya is strange, mysterious and indescribable. We cannot say what it is, but from its effects we can infer its existence. Its essential nature cannot be understood. Only its effects can be seen, but its effects can be destroyed when we realize Brahman.

Maya does its work through the three gunas, the three tendencies in nature, and in the world of existence. They are rajas, tamas and sattva. The power of rajas is unceasing activity. In humanity it is manifested as lust, anger, greed, malice, arrogance, jealousy and envy. In nature it is manifested as constant growth and change. The power of tamas is ignorance, laziness, dullness, slothfulness and delusion when manifested in humanity. In nature it is manifested as immobility and heaviness. The power of sattva when mixed with the influence of rajas and tamas is manifested as self-discipline, reverence, the doing of good works, and desire for liberation. In its pure state sattva becomes the means of humanity's liberation from maya. It is characterized by purity, tranquility, contentment, cheerfulness and by concentration on the task of gaining liberation.

The Atman sees all, but no one sees it. It pervades the whole universe. The body functions at its command. It is pure consciousness, in a state of absolute joy. The Atman is unborn and deathless, not subject to growth and decay. It is unchangeable and eternal, and is not destroyed when the body is destroyed. Realize that the Atman is the true Self, and realize the truth of its identity with Brahman.

Confusion of appearance with reality causes one to think that a snake is a piece of rope. The confusion is caused by the power of rajas and tamas. They cause us to think that the body is the real Self.

Encased in the five sheaths produced by maya the Atman remains hidden. But when the sheaths are removed what remains is Atman. The physical body is first of the five sheaths. The subtle body is the second. The mental body is the third. The sense of ego is the fourth, and the intellect is the fifth.

The intellect has its own brilliance and reflects the joy of the Atman. But it still has a sense of ego and is subject to ignorance. Because of its proximity to Atman some may confuse it with Atman, but it is not so. The Atman is pure consciousness."

The Student asks, "When the five sheaths are removed, then surely nothing is left but void?"

The Guru replies, "Not so, there is something remaining which is aware of the void. This thing that remains is the Atman. The Atman sees all changeable things but is itself unchanged. Realize this deep in your heart.

Realize also that Atman is Brahman, and Brahman is Atman, and that Brahman alone is real. The Upanishads have long emphasized the identity of Brahman and Atman. Remind yourself of it by continual repetition of the phrase, Tat Tvam Asi, You Are It.

Brahman may be looked on as God, creator of the universe.

Atman may be looked on as the individual soul with its five sheaths. Seen thus they appear to be separate, but this is merely the effect of maya. Neither God nor Soul are real when the effects of maya are removed. Brahman is not the phenomenal universe. Again, we mistake the snake for the rope.

Realize that the utterance 'You Are It' takes you beyond class, nation, family and race. It takes you beyond the range of speech, and beyond all human infirmities, beyond all mental concepts, and beyond cause and effect. Realize that 'You Are It'.

As you become increasingly devoted to realizing the Atman worldliness and its desires fall away. It becomes like a dream, without reality. The mind of the yogi dissolves, desires disappear and only Atman remains.

The quality of tamas are eliminated by the qualities of rajas and sattva. The qualities of rajas are removed by sattva in its mixed nature, and sattva in its mixed nature by sattva in its pure form.

Realize the unreality of manifested things. The universe is unreal, and our own ego is unreal because they are constantly changing. So cease to identify with name and form, with family and profession, society and nations, even with your actions and thoughts, for Atman is above action and thought.

The ego is a large poisonous snake, and the three gunas are its heads. It is coiled round the treasure which is the bliss of Brahman. With the sword of spiritual knowledge cut off the three heads, and win the treasure. Even the most ascetic yogi cannot gain liberation so long as ego remains.

There must be no negligence in devotion to Brahman. Constantly turn your thoughts to Brahman. If the mind turns to sense objects craving starts, and a hundred distractions appear. The Yajur Veda has said that one is subject to fear as long as one feels separated from Brahman. In hundreds of ancient writings it has been emphasized that ego has no real existence. Sorrow will come to those who do not realize this. The ego is delusion produced by maya. Cut it away if you would be emancipated from changeful existence.

Through the experience of samadhi the sense of separateness disappears. Only those who have experienced it are free from ignorance. As gold is refined by fire and purged of dross, so the mind must purge itself of the dross of rajas, tamas and sattva if it is to be free from ignorance.

By experience of samadhi desire falls away, and one becomes free of karma. To reflect on the truth of Brahman is a hundred times better than to hear or read about it. And to meditate on it is a hundred thousand times better. But to experience it in samadhi is best of all. Only in nirvikalpa samadhi can the true nature of Brahman be revealed.

The first gate of yoga is control of speech. Then non-acceptance of unnecessary gifts. Then absence of any expectation of reward. Then absence of desire. And finally devotion to Brahman. Uninterrupted devotion to Brahman leads to cessation of sense enjoyment. This leads to tranquility, and this leads to destruction of the ego. Thence proceeds the yogi's enjoyment of the bliss of Brahman.

Detachment from what is inner, and what is outer can only be achieved by one who has renounced body, senses, ego, mind and intellect. Outer renunciation is to sense objects. Inner renunciation is to the ego. One needs discrimination and detachment as a bird needs two wings to fly. Without them the top of the tree of liberation cannot be reached.

Keep the sense organs in their proper place. Prevent them from roving. Keep the body steady and firm, not troubled overmuch about its wellbeing. And being absorbed in the Atman realize the bliss of Brahman. The Atman is Brahman. It is within and without, before and behind. It is north and south, east and west. This whole existence is really pure consciousness, and the real self is Supreme Brahman.

We drink the wine of maya, become deluded, and instead of unity see separateness. But there is no duality in Brahman, the all-pervading infinite. What else remains to be known? What else is there to say?

The yogi, the ascetic who lives in the eternal bliss of knowledge of the Atman is said to be a jivanmukti. With such the objective universe is almost forgotten. Though awake he appears to be dreaming. He is free of even the faintest traces of desire. He no longer even thinks. He is devoid of ego and the consciousness of possession. He is concerned with neither past, present nor future. He looks on everything as equal. He looks on the agreeable and the disagreeable with equal mind.

He is indifferent to what happens to his body. He lives only in the bliss of Atman.

Although the jivanmukti lives on because of past karma, that karma was extinguished on his realizing Brahman. Yet the body will live out its life in this world. To any but the unenlightened he will appear like everyone else. But to those who have achieved wisdom he will be recognized as one who has achieved illumination in this life. Thus in the jivanmukti the results of past karma will continue to work themselves out in body and mind. The residual power of karma will continue as long as he lives. Thus when it is all played out the body will drop away, and the liberated one will never take another."

The disciple, who had attended closely to the guru's words, went away to meditate, reason and reflect again on the ancient writings. He withdrew all senses from sense objects. He remained with body straight, and steady as a rock, completely absorbed in Brahman. Then on returning to normal consciousness he was overwhelmed by a great feeling of joy. He returned to the guru and said:

"I have been in union with Brahman. All I know is bliss, but not its extent or limits. What I feel cannot be described. Just as a hailstone falls into the sea, so I am merged into this vast ocean of joy. The world has gone. That which I perceived exists no more. I am indifferent to everything, and only know I am Atman, pure consciousness, pure joy.

By your grace and guidance I have achieved my object; the goal of all life and existence. I have found the Atman. I am without attachment, and without body. I am sexless and indestructible, calm, infinite and without strain.

I am neither doer nor enjoyer, without change and without action. I am neither this nor that, neither within nor without. Like space I go further than thought. Like a mountain I am immovable. Like the ocean I am boundless. I am the Atman, Self-illumined and infinite.

Once more I salute you, O guru. In your great compassion you have awoken me from my sleep of ignorance. You have saved me from ever more roaming in the dreamlike forest of birth, old age and death: this universe created by maya, ruled by the three gunas, and forever afflicted by pain, fear and suffering."

The guru speaks to the assembled disciples: "See my

friends how this devotee has found the joy of Atman in samadhi, and awakened forever to consciousness of reality. Our perception of the universe is really a glimpse of Brahman. We are in touch with Brahman constantly, but we do not realize it. When the moon shines in full glory do we prefer to see a picture instead? When you can experience the bliss of Brahman would you wish for anything less? The Atman is pure consciousness, joyful and silent. Bathe yourself in the great peace of this silence, and enjoy eternal bliss.

When one has found this perfect tranquility he no longer needs sacred places, moral disciplines, rituals, postures, prayers, or objects of meditation. His knowledge of Atman does not depend on any special times or conditions. Atman shines with its own light. Nothing in the whole of existence can reveal it. Existence is only because of the Atman, so how can any existent thing reveal it.

He who has seen the Atman is free of limitations, because he delights only in the Atman. The needs of his life, food, shelter and sustenance come to him without effort. He lives free and unfettered. He sleeps without fear, and eats and clothes himself as he will. Though past karma continues to work itself out in his body he is unaffected by it. He is untouched by pleasure and pain, evil or good. He has gone beyond them all.

The ignorant seeing a jivanmukti will judge him by his body, speech or clothes, and will honour or despise him accordingly. But the enlightened one will be unaffected, completely detached from it all. And when the time comes to vacate the body he will let it fall where it will, completely unconcerned.

One who achieves liberation in life, also achieves it in death, and is never again reborn.

Now I have revealed to you the supreme teaching, the Crest Jewel of all the ancient writings. I regard you as my very own son. Now go in peace and joy."

May this dialogue between guru and disciple inspire others who seek this liberation. May these words of Sankara crown their efforts with success.'

It is clear on reading the Viveka Chudamani that at the time of Sankara the ideas enshrined in the older Upanishads were now well established. In Vedanta very little of the older Vedic thought remains; it is almost entirely that of yoga and samkhya. The Atman-Brahman doctrine, and that of reincarnation and karma first tentatively promulgated in the oldest of Upanishads, the Brihadaranyaka, is now spoken of by Sankara as established Hindu doctrine. The samkhya ideas of purusha and prakriti, the three gunas, and of maya are spoken of in familiar terms. The Six Systems of Philosophy are mentioned, and yoga practice is emphasized throughout.

The clarity of Sankara's thought is well illustrated in his treatment of the concept of maya. It is a difficult concept, which he makes almost understandable. He also clarifies the action of the three gunas, the baleful effect of tamas, and the misleading effect of rajas. Moreover his teaching on mixed and pure sattva is most enlightening. References to Buddhist doctrines are notably absent, but Sankara was probably at pains to play down any Buddhist ideas.

The Viveka Chudamani represents yet another synthesis in the syncretistic tradition of India. It is a very clear and satisfying synthesis, and brings Vedanta right up to date. Vedanta is still substantially in the form that Sankara left it 1,200 years ago.

CHAPTER 11
Laya Yoga

Meditation is the very heart of yoga. Sitting quietly, and just thinking about a situation, a person, a project or a problem is the simplest form of meditation. It can be practised by anyone sufficiently calm and self-disciplined not to feel the need for constant stimulation from some outside source, or from evoking past memories or desires. From this simple form of meditation, which is highly beneficial from its effect of both stimulating and relaxing at the same time, other forms have developed. Patanjali differentiates in his sutras between meditation with seed and meditation without seed. The latter is difficult and comes to very few even after much effort. The mind has to be kept completely blank. This is contrary to one's nature, but is used in the final stages of samadhi.

In meditation with seed an object of some kind is meditated on. The simplest object may be a flower, a picture, a statue or a symbol. Anything that will both quieten and inspire one. In tantrism, as we have seen, this classical yoga type of meditation became more active, taking the form of a ritual, with aids of various kinds, such as the intoning of mantras, the playing of music, garlanding of statues, and even dancing. Apart from this there is meditation on one's own nature. The early Buddhist meditation on a rotting corpse is one such, rather bizarre meditation, meant to make us realize our own mortality and the transitoriness of life. There is however something morbid, egotistical and hypochondriac about any meditation on our selves. Yet such an exercise can be beneficial if undertaken in a creative way.

It seems to have been a need to discover some creative way of meditating on our own nature that prompted the development of laya yoga in the first place: some way that would cause the imagination to move outwards from an inward starting point. The distinctive form of meditation which is laya yoga has been remarkably popular, and continues to grow in importance. It is a form of yoga that developed without reference to religion. Like hatha yoga later it was entirely a secular development. As with yoga generally its beginnings must have been out of actual experience. When sitting for meditation, and in entering the ecstatic state of samadhi, many practitioners must have felt a vivid sense of energy rising from the base of the spine, with a cleansing and vitalising effect on the whole system, finally manifesting itself as a burst of energy coming through the top of the head. This experience is rare today, but by no means unknown. It is quite possible that in earlier times it was fairly common.

Given that this basic experience, the rousing of the kundalini force as it is called, was genuine and not imagined, how did the elaborate scheme of the centres of energy, the chakras, and their associated nadis, or energy pathways come into being? As neither chakras nor nadis can be seen we have to conclude that they could be sensed in some other way. This could be some kind of clairvoyance, perhaps coupled with deep trance. Some modern clairvoyants claim to see the chakras, and some dowsers are said to be able to locate them with a pendulum. Assuming that they exist what is so remarkable about them that this highly specialized form of yoga has developed?

One answer may well be that at the time of the earliest mentions of the kundalini force yoga was moving in the direction of healing. It was using the well-established yoga techniques to activate, sedate or generally heal the body and mind of those sufficiently advanced in the technique to respond to the instructions of a guru who would be leading them in their meditation. Yoga was forming links with Ayurvedic medicine, and indeed many Ayurvedic doctors were very advanced yogis themselves. They were beginning to use yoga as a therapy in its own right, and like the meridians and points in acupuncture, that we cannot see but know to exist, these yogic physicians took to experimenting with this extremely subtle energy system.

The principal object of laya yoga is to use meditative techniques to cleanse and activate this energy system, and bring it into balance. When combined with the known

benefits of pranayama this may well become a very potent
system of preventive medicine. A full kundalini meditation
will make use of mantric sounds as well as pranayama and the
visualizations of the chakras. Each chakra has a dominant,
and certain sub-dominant mantric sounds associated with it.
The total number comes to fifty. This corresponds to the
number of letters and sounds in the Sanskrit alphabet, so the
number is not arbitrary. The origins of Sanskrit (the elder
sister of Greek and Latin) are unknown, but it is claimed in
India to have been divinely given, with each letter and its
corresponding sound relating to an aspect of man's nature.

In the same way that a mantric sound is associated with
each chakra so also with pranayama. There is a particular
breathing exercise associated with each chakra. So in a full-
scale kundalini meditation attention will be focused on a
particular chakra, the relevant breathing exercise will be
performed, and the relevant mantra will be intoned. The
effect of all this, if not actually to raise kundalini, is to feel a
great restorative calm rise up within the spinal column,
activating the organs connected with each chakra. It is
probably this restorative effect which has been used to heal
many diseased conditions of mind and body. Certainly the
whole system is intriguing and stimulating in its richness of
imagery and in the complexity of its execution. It has
considerable potential for further development.

Although laya yoga reached its full flowering in the tantric
period it was known much earlier. References can be found in
the puranas, principally the Shivapurana, Brahmawaiwarta-
purana, Dewibhagavata, Skandapurana, Lingapurana, Bha-
gavata and Kalikapurana. These references, however, are
only fragmentary hints and guesses at their significance. In
some of the later Upanishads, by such writers as Narayana
and Makeswara, fuller descriptions are found. These are
Yogachudamani Upanishad, and Yogarajopanishad.

These early descriptions are of interest only to the scholar.
The tantric is the system in universal use. Even today it is by
no means complete. Each leading exponent will put a greater
or lesser emphasis here and there depending on his own
experience. This is also because the balance of the chakras is
different for each individual. Some are dominant, some
almost dormant. The main chakra systems are those

expounded by the tantric masters Shiwa, Bhairawi, Rishi Narada, Mahidhara, Brahmananda, Jnananand, Lakshmana, Deshikendra and Brahmananda Giri.

It may help at this point to define some terms. Laya yoga is that branch of yoga, which has as its main emphasis a method of concentration using the chakra system. It also involves concentration on and understanding of the nadis, which are fine lines of energy running round and through the chakras and various organs of the body. The ultimate objective is to raise the kundalini force which resides in the lowest chakra, the muladhara. By the concentration exercises of laya yoga this kundalini energy, said to lie in the form of a coiled serpent, is aroused to the point at which it spontaneously moves up the spinal cord, activating each of the chakras in turn, until it reaches the highest, sahasrara. Each chakra is the focus of a particular type of energy. Chakra means a wheel, and clairvoyants claim to have seen the chakras spinning with energy like a wheel. Attempts have been made to equate nadis with nerves, and chakras with particular organs. These have not been successful, except that some connection with the endocrine glands seems to be a possibility.

The tantric scheme describes seven main chakras. For most concentration and meditation purposes these provide a sufficiently rich storehouse of meaning. But there are several minor chakras. These are hrit, below the heart, talu at the level of the nose, manas and indu just above ajna, and nirvana and guru associated with sahasrara, which itself lies outside the body. So the full scheme of major and minor chakras makes thirteen.

Muladhara is the basal chakra. It is situated in the region below the genitals and above the anus, and is attached to the mouth of the sushumna nadi. The sushumna is the main nadi, running right up the centre of the spine.

Svadisthana is the second chakra. It lies in the region of the genitals, and is joined to the sushumna nadi.

Manipura is the third chakra. It is situated in the region of the solar plexus, and is also joined to the sushumna nadi.

Hrit is a minor chakra associated with Anahata. It also is joined to the sushumna nadi.

Anahata is the fourth chakra and is joined to the sushumna

nadi. It is located on the spine at the level of the heart.

Vishuddha is the fifth chakra and is joined to the sushumna nadi. It is situated in the neck.

Talu is a minor chakra situated in the upper part of the cervical spinal column.

Ajna is the sixth chakra, and is joined to the sushumna nadi. It is located in the forehead between the eyebrows.

Manas is a minor chakra joined to the sushumna nadi. It is associated with ajna.

Indu is a minor chakra situated within the sushumna nadi, and also associated with ajna.

Nirvana is a minor chakra. It is joined to the sushumna nadi and associated with sahasrara. It is the last chakra to be joined to the sushumna nadi which ends here, just within the cranium.

Guru is a minor chakra, and is the lower aspect of the sahasrara. It is situated between the top of the cranium and sahasrara.

Sahasrara is the last chakra, and lies just above the head. It is not attached to any nadi.

Along with the main sushumna nadi are two others, ida and pingala. Ida is on the left and pingala on the right of sushumna. They start at muladhara and end at ajna. They move around the chakras on their upward course in a semi-circular way, moving left to right, then right to left. There are said to be thousands of minor nadis, but only these three are recognized for kundalini meditation. It is interesting to note that the symbol of the medical profession, the caduceus, whose origin is unknown is in fact a representation of the three major nadis, while the wings at the top are the sahasrara chakra.

The symbology of the chakras is quite complex. Each has a centre formed by a circle, with a number of petals arranged round it. Colours of both centre and petals vary in each case. At the tip of each petal or at the centre of the circle is a Sanskrit letter, which is also a mantric sound. When the mantric sounds of each chakra are intoned and the chakra visualized then the specific energies of the chakra are invoked. There are further shapes within each centre circle: triangles, circles and squares, and within them again may be the sexual symbols of lingam and yoni. Associated with each chakra is a concentration form of one of the gods of the Hindu pantheon. These are separate and additional pictures heavy with symbolism. They appear to be traditional artists' representations of the powers of each chakra elaborated to include humans and animals in a pleasing picture helpful to those not able to use the chakras in the intense concentrative way undertaken by laya yogis. Without considerable knowledge of the Hindu pantheon, and unless thoroughly versed in Indian traditions one could never arrive at a satisfactory understanding of these pictures. We shall therefore consider only the chakras themselves, and proceed to describe each one.

The muladhara chakra has four petals blood red in colour, on each of the four is a Sanskrit letter. The colour of the centre of the circle is yellow. Inside it is a square of deeper yellow, and inside that a square of deep red. Inside the triangle is a lingam coloured deep blue.

The svadisthana chakra has six petals coloured vermilion. On each petal is a Sanskrit letter. The centre circle is pale yellow. Inside it is a white semi-circle containing the letter Wang.

The manipura chakra has ten petals coloured dark green or blue, each with a Sanskrit letter. The centre circle is pale yellow, and contains a red triangle pointing downward. The triangle has an entry point at each side, and contains a Sanskrit letter.

The hrit chakra has eight petals deep gold in colour. At the centre are three concentric circles representing the sun region, vermilion, the moon region, white, and the fire region, deep red. Within the inner circle is a tree with a yogi seated beneath it.

The anahata chakra has twelve petals each containing a Sanskrit letter. The colour is deep red. The centre circle is pale yellow containing a six pointed star, within which is the Sanskrit letter Yang. At one point of the star is a smaller triangle containing a red coloured lingam and yoni.

The vishuddha chakra has sixteen petals of deep smoke colour. The centre circle is pale yellow containing a further circle pale smoke in colour. This contains a downward pointing triangle, within which is another circle containing the Sanskrit letter Hang.

The talu chakra has twelve red petals, and outside them a further sixty-four white ones. The centre circle is red and within it is a further circle which is white.

The ajna chakra has two white petals each containing a Sanskrit letter. The centre circle is pale yellow. Within it is a downward pointing triangle coloured pale smoke containing the Sanskrit letter Ong. Above the triangle is a white half moon, and above that the golden circle of the sun.

The indu chakra has sixteen white petals. The centre circle is a white moon region and within that a nine-cornered region containing a swan. Superimposed on the swan is the Hindu god Parashiva and his shakti Siddhakali.

The nirvana chakra has one hundred white petals. Within the centre circle are horizontal bands coloured green, blue, black, yellow and white.

The guru chakra has twelve white petals. The centre circle is also white. It contains a downward facing triangle also white, with Sanskrit letters arranged around each side and within each point. Within the triangle is a white circle containing a picture of a guru with his shakti.

The sahasrara chakra has one thousand petals in twenty layers of fifty each. The petals are in changing colours of white, red, yellow, black and green. The centre circle is pale yellow containing a further circle of pale blue, within which is an upward pointing triangle coloured gold, with a red dot in the centre.

The nadis have not received the same attention as the chakras. We have already said that there are considered to be thousands of them, but two hundred are considered important. Of these fourteen are principal nadis. These are sushumna, ida, pingala, gandhari, hasthajihva, kuhu, saraswati, pusha, sankhini, paysawini, varuni, alambhusha, vishvodhara and yasavini. Chitrini, which is within sushumna is not a nadi in the same sense as the others. Ida to the left of the spinal cord is female, lunar, passive and pale. Pingala to the right is male, positive, solar and red. They ascend with circular motion up the spine, round the chakras, but not through them, and join sushumna at the ajna chakra making a

triple knot, then end at the left and right nostril respectively.
Thus control of breath through one or other nostril will
affect our nature, making it more male and positive, or
female and negative at certain times. An interesting yogic
observation is that in most cases the right nostril is more open
in the morning, up to noon. The situation then gradually
changes and the left nostril is more open in the afternoon. It
is considered necessary to have both nostrils completely open
and balanced in higher meditation.

Whereas traditionally the whole scheme of chakras, nadis
and the kundalini force were referred to as laya yoga, today
laya and kundalini are often referred to as separate meditations. In laya yoga one visualizes prana being drawn
downwards into the body through the fontanelle at the top of
the head. In kundalini yoga energy is brought upwards from
the basal chakra. In practice the feeling of each is quite
different. In laya yoga there is a cooling, spiritual quality to
the process. In kundalini yoga the first emotion as the energy
at the base of the spine is activated is one of turgid
restlessness. Only gradually is this feeling modified as the
visualization rises through the various chakras, becoming
more spiritualized as it rises. It gains in power as it rises by becoming more subtle, and is finally said to burst through the
sahasrara as a great shower of multicoloured sparks.

Although attempts to equate the system with the organs
and systems of the physical body have not been successful
some authorities feel that the system externalizes itself as the
endocrine system, but that the chakras and nadis belong to
the etheric body and no exact correspondence can be mapped
out. Nevertheless as our nature is formed by the balance of
these and other systems so our nature can be determined by
the energies and emotions mediated through the chakras.
The following is the broad outline of these emotional
tendencies.

Muladhara is concerned with the most basic instinct of all,
self-preservation. It is the earth chakra, that is, it earths one.
It is concerned with our animal nature as an earth being. It
links us to nature and the soil. It is concerned with survival
and the fact of being. It has the adrenals, the fight or flight
glands associated with it. Muladhara also regulates the senses

of taste and smell. Kundalini is the vital force asleep in it.

Svadisthana is associated with the prostatic plexus, the lumbar region, the gonads, the sex urge, the procreative drive. Because people would not necessarily procreate by choice nature has made the process extremely pleasurable. The pleasure principle residing in this chakra extends to pleasure generally. So this is the centre for pleasurable addiction to food and drugs and material comfort. Escapism into the fantasy world of fiction and entertainment also come within the scope of this chakra.

Manipura is concerned with ego, with one's opinion of oneself. In most people this chakra is strong, and a high proportion spend their lives strengthening it. It is all about being identified as someone special, and is concerned with will power and ambition. In most people these first three chakras function together. If one is strong all three tend to be strong. If one is weak all three tend to be weak. Energy moves freely between then. Nature has supplied these as our basic equipment, and the forces associated with them are of this basic nature. The gland associated with the manipura is the pancreas. It also rules the solar plexus and the epigastric plexus. Manipura regulates digestion and physical wellbeing and gives physical strength. Many very strong men have strong development of the stomach muscles in the solar plexus area.

Anahata is the heart centre. It is associated with the thymus gland and the cardiac plexus. With this fourth chakra we move into a more spiritual realm, with corresponding emotions. The uppermost emotion here is that of love or compassion for all beings. With this chakra is associated the sense of touch. It is difficult to express love for a human being or animal without touching or hugging them. The energy residing in the three lower chakras can be sublimated in the fourth. So we admire people through history who have managed to do this. Some people have this chakra so highly developed that it functions at the expense of all the others. Even the functions of the three lower chakras seem to be suspended. Such people are saints, but it can also be said that some of them are addicts. They are addicted to 'do-gooding', and receive considerable ego satisfaction in this way. Some also do it because they know of no other way to survive. The heart centre is usually the first to which the student will be directed by his guru.

Vishuddha rules the thyroid gland and the laryngeal plexus. It is concerned with communication, the spoken word, with study and the search for truth. Science and scholarship are developed at this chakra. Sometimes it is strongly connected with the lower chakra when the search for truth is carried on in an impassioned way to benefit mankind. A lot of science and technology starts out this way, but we are having doubts about their value. Sometimes this chakra leads people into dogmatism. The next one above it needs activating, or perhaps the third chakra ruling the ego sense is too strong. Vishuddha is the seat of creativity, and of sound and speech.

Ajna is the sixth chakra. It rules the pineal and pituitary glands, and is the seat of intelligence and insight. Intelligence gives one an overview of the world. Insight goes even further. Within the term insight are included psychic powers, known in classical yoga as siddhis. Great stress is laid on opening up this chakra gradually. Complete control of the lower chakras, and having them in balance is considered essential. If one does not have conscious control of the lower chakras while opening up the ajna the result can be disorientation of various kinds. The powers of the lower chakras can go out of control, resulting in obsession and other derangements. Ideally the ajna is opened up with the aid of a guru. If there is no guru then the correct way is to strive to get the lower chakras in balance, and wait for the ajna to open naturally.

Psychic powers manifested spontaneously can be the result of work carried out on oneself in a previous incarnation. Otherwise any unbalanced manifestation is considered morbid, and a psychic of this kind is more deserving of curiosity than of respect.

Sahasrara is not associated with any gland or part of the nervous system. It exists outside the body above the top of the head. While insight is a feature of the ajna a more spiritual kind of insight is associated with the sahasrara. This is the world of the mystic. It is also the domain of spiritual power. This power is a part of the greater power of the cosmos. It can be tapped and drawn down to spiritualize each chakra in turn. It is our contact with spirit, just as the muladhara is our contact with earth.

A laya yoga or kundalini meditation done alone is rarely successful. It is far more beneficial to have a group leader to talk a group through the chakra system. One then meditates in response to their stimulus. As the powers and character-istics of each one are dilated on the student will be measuring himself against this yardstick, and becomes aware of his deficiencies and excesses. Group healing is also done when a person is very imbalanced in one of the chakras. The group then concentrates on the chakra concerned, feeling its powers within themselves, and intoning its principal mantra. A modern development is the application of the radiesthetic sense to checking imbalances in the chakras. Medical dowsers using a blood spot or lock of hair from the person concerned claim to be able to discover imbalances in the chakras using a pendulum or radionic instrument. They then treat the person at a distance by beaming the relevant colour for each chakra onto the sample. These practitioners claim to be treating the physical body via the etheric body. Their results are impress-ive, even though the techniques seem very unusual.

The chakras are foci of pranic energy. They can be looked on as transformers of this energy. The main control point for harnessing this energy is at the point where the three main nadis, ida, pingala and sushumna join in a triple knot. This is at the left and right nostrils and is said to be under the direct control of the ajna chakra. Thus control of breath, which has always been so important in yoga is given greater clarification and meaning in laya yoga. The circulation of prana within the body is said to be affected by the time of day, the phases of the moon, and by the conjunction of the stars at any one time. So prana itself varies in quality, being more beneficial in the morning and less so during the day, although there is an increase at noon, and another in the early evening. Prana is spoken of as a universal energy which is all-pervading, but is more concentrated at certain places, e.g. the tops of moun-tains, or near running water. Some correspondences have been discovered here with concentrations of negative ions in such places. Prana has often been likened to electricity.

It can be demonstrated physiologically that at the region of each chakra there is always a concentration of nervous tissue. At the muladhara is a massive concentration of nerves and blood vessels. The fact that nerves carry a charge of electricity is now well established. It may be that negative ions are concentrated at the chakra points, and that they are released when the heavy charge of static electricity at the base of the spine is discharged. In further support of this theory is the fact that this basal region is the body's discharge area, i.e. of urine, faeces and semen. These discharges are accompanied by emotions varying from relief to ecstasy. The release of kundalini is described in similar terms, and often accompanied by a thorough psychic and emotional cleansing culminating in samadhi. The body is often, but not always, left physically reinvigorated.

A modern authority, Gopi Krishna, experienced the raising of kundalini in 1937 after seventeen years of regular meditation on the sahasrara chakra. He has spent the rest of his life researching the subject, and putting forth a constant stream of literature. The experience in his own words was as follows:

> The illumination grew brighter, the roaring louder and louder. I experienced a rocking sensation and then felt myself slipping out of my body, entirely enveloped in a halo of light. I felt the point of consciousness that was myself growing wider, surrounded by waves of light. I was now all consciousness, without any outline, without any idea of a corporeal appendage, without any feeling or sensation coming from the senses, immersed in a sea of light, simultaneously conscious and aware of every point, spread out, as it were in all directions without any barrier or material obstructions. I was a vast circle of awareness in which the body was but a point, bathed in light and in a state of exultation impossible to describe.

The result of this kundalini arousal was that Gopi Krishna was ill for years afterwards, being near to death several times, but gradually he got better. In 1949 he began to experience a series of most blissful trance states of mystical awareness. This was marked by a sudden outpouring of mystical poetry, which he had never written before, first in Kashmiri, his native language, then in English and Punjabi, both of which were familiar to him. These were followed to his great amazement by verses in Persian, Urdu, of which he knew very little, and German, French and Italian, of which languages he claimed that he had no knowledge.

At this time he felt in touch with a reservoir of all knowledge, and felt that all he had to do was to wish and whatever he wanted to know would be given to him. The same feeling has been described by yogis and mystics down the ages. This was Gopi Krishna's awakening of the kundalini force. In his later writings he appeals for more research, and more competent teachers, so that this latent energy can be tapped and utilized by all in a safe and controlled manner. This he sees as one of the next great adventures for mankind.

CHAPTER 12
Tibetan Yoga

Buddhism, and with it yoga, came to Tibet originally around AD 500, but made little impact. In 617 Sron-Btsan-Gampo was born who became king of Tibet and in 638 and 641 married princesses from Nepal and China. Both were Buddhists, and brought their own priests, books and images with them. They eventually converted the king, which caused him to despatch a leading monk, Thon-mi-Sambhota, with sixteen other monks to South India to collect principal Buddhist texts. Sambhota also created a Tibetan alphabet based on Sanskrit. King Sron-Btsan made Buddhism the official religion over Bon, the popular religion of the time. He built many temples including the Potala at Lhasa. In spite of his efforts, however, the people still maintained their allegiance to Bon.

A situation similar to that in China then developed. The people began to practise both religions, or perhaps practised one and paid lip-service to the other. In China it has long been common practice for people to be Confucian, Taoist and also Buddhist, a situation baffling to the West, who have been brought up within the Christian context which asserts that only one religion can be true, and only that can command our allegiance.

The works translated by Sambhota were of the Yogacara school, so from this early introduction of Buddhism yoga influence was strong. But it was a philosophical and intellectual influence, not of a kind to appeal to the common people. Yogacara taught ten stages of spiritual development before Buddhahood is reached. Pure consciousness is the ultimate reality. Only mind was real, and thought is all-powerful. We have already seen that it introduced an esoteric element into Mahayana, and provided the philosophical framework for tantrism. It was therefore a practical philosophy based on yoga and tantrism. It criticized the Upanishads as too intellectual, and Theravada Buddhism (Hinayana) as too moralistic to provide a sound foundation on which men and women could live to the full and realize their latent powers. It held that knowledge alone was insufficient. One must go on to personal experience and practical realization.

In spite of these yogic, tantric and esoteric elements Buddhism still failed to make progress, so a later king, Ti-Song-De-tsen, invited the leading teacher of tantrism at the university of Nalanda to visit the country. This was Padma Sambhava, professor of yoga and esoteric studies at this great Buddhist foundation. Nalanda in the north of Bengal was by all accounts a very large institution, bigger than many modern universities. It was to have considerable influence on the spread of Buddhism into China later on, but was eventually sacked by the Moslems in the eleventh century.

Padma Sambhava arrived in 747 and stayed for the rest of his life. He quickly established his authority by first exorcizing some spirits believed to be causing earthquakes in a certain part of the country. It is recorded that no further earthquakes occurred after this exorcism. He then went on to beat a Bon opponent in a public display of magic. We are not told of what the display consisted.

Although Padma Sambhava and his teaching became popular the indigenous Bon religion still maintained its hold over the people, and in order to make Buddhism more acceptable he arranged a series of compromises. He added many of the Bon rites and deities and many of its most recondite theories and practices. The result was a rich mixture of metaphysics, mysticism, magic and occultism, all held together by a considerable emphasis on yoga practice. Bon opposition was intense for well over a century, but out of this ordeal of opposition and compromise came many innovations. Some of these have had a lasting influence on yoga, and provided an impetus that has carried this mixture of Bon and tantra into the present era. This body of doctrine and practice came to be gathered together and formalized later as the Ningmapa school of Tantric Buddhism, although Padma Sambhava referred to his system as Adi-yoga.

Such was the impact of Padma Sambhava on the cultural life of Tibet that subsequent generations have elevated him to the status of a god. He became known as Guru Rimpoche, the glorious, teacher and also referred to without naming him, as the lotus-born. He is featured in many Tibetan tankas surrounded by disciples, boddhisattvas and minor gods. A tanka is a Tibetan mandala, and seems to be one of the elements taken over from Bon. Mandalas are symbolic pictures. The drawing of mandalas became a very fine art. Many of them are exceedingly detailed and ornate. They include archetypal symbols from the deepest layers of the sub-conscious mind. Carl Gustav Jung, the eminent psychiatrist, made some of his more psychotic patients draw whatever came into their heads. He found that they produced many of the symbols found on Tibetan tankas, which led him to infer that these various symbols belong to different layers of consciousness, and are as real to the human personality as limbs are to the body. He coined the word 'archetype' for these shapes and symbols in relevant colours, and found that an improvement could be discerned in the patient who drew shapes belonging to a more normal level of the mind.

Tibetan mandalas use five colours, each representing a direction, and occurring at certain points in the general design. They are: white – east, yellow – south, red – west, green – north, blue – centre. The tanka is square, with each side as long as the distance from the elbow to the end of the middle finger. One's own personal tanka is of this size. There is always a blue circle in the centre. It is both a concentrator and a stimulator, and is used to invoke the powers incorporated into it when first drawn. The drawing of mandalas is a valuable yoga exercise, and is being used more and more as the energies in them become better understood.

Padma Sambhava founded the first order of monks, the seniors being known as Lamas. Thus Lamaism is a term used by many to describe the typically Tibetan form of religious organization. The adi-yoga doctrines of Padma Sambhava were augmented after his death, and became a very extensive body of doctrine known as the 'Great Perfection System'. It has been compared in scope with the 'Encyclopaedia Britannica' and was edited by Long-Chen Rab-Jampa. The Rab-Jampa is a Lamaist degree roughly equivalent to a European degree of doctor of divinity. The knowledge displayed in the

Great Perfection System is rather different from the knowledge relevant to our own time, but not very unlike that of the European early middle ages, with which it was contemporary. Thus astrology and the occult sciences were represented, as well as medicine, the physical sciences and the arts. Geomancy and exorcism were also present, and among the more interesting and gruesome of the rites and ceremonies was the Chod rite.

This elaborate ceremony was taken over from Bon and adapted to bring home to the devotee the truth that the body is impermanent, and once life has left it returns to the elements very quickly, and not in a nice and ordered fashion. The ceremony is carried out at a cremation ground or at the place where bodies are put out for dismemberment by birds and wild animals. This is the usual way of disposing bodies in Tibet. The rite is enacted as a ritual dance, the steps of which have to be learned by heart. While he dances, the devotee recites the prayers and mantras of the rite. He carries a bell, a dorje (staff), a dagger, a drum and a trumpet made from a human femur. He first blows the trumpet to call all the demons of the underworld to come to the feast – the human body. Then he begins to dance and intone the prayers and mantras, gradually speeding up the whole ritual until he is almost in a frenzy. The object is to subdue all the forces he has called up in himself. To dance among the bones and corpses is to bring home to the devotee the dark side of life and of death more vividly than would be possible sitting comfortably trying to imagine the same thing. The rite must be enacted alone, and at dead of night. Some of its practitioners make extended tours into India, Nepal and Mongolia seeking out suitable places. Chod is one of the many rites pertaining to the 'Short Path' to nirvana. The object of the short path is to obtain enlightenment in the present incarnation, so that one does not return except by choice as a boddhisattva. Some of the extreme tantric yogis spend their whole lives performing this rite, and travelling far in its practice.

The preoccupation with death in the Chod rite, and so much a part of Tibetan thinking, found its most distinctive expression in one of the great yoga classics, unique in world literature. This is the Bardo Thodol, or the Tibetan Book of the Dead. There are in fact several Tibetan books of the dead, ranging from the Bardo Thodol, a lengthy manual in seventeen chapters, to small booklets to be carried on the person. They are often in the form of mandalas within which are written the basic mantras, so condensed that they can contain in a few pages of 'mantric shorthand' the whole essence of the Bardo Thodol.

There have been other books of the dead. The Egyptian is well known, and the Garuda Purana of Hinduism served the same purpose. They have existed in other cultures, but none have the modernity and explicitness of the Tibetan. The others were manuals for priests only, whereas the Bardo Thodol is for anyone able to practise yoga. The Bardo Thodol (bardo means the limbo state between lives, thodol means the teachings) describes what happens after death, the events in the bardo, and what happens during the preparation for a new birth. When used by a priest, or a relative, or a guru known to the dead or dying person certain of the relevant mantras will be intoned. This reading or intoning of mantras can go on for forty-nine days, though in most cases for only fourteen days. The yoga understanding of the after-death state is that the messages contained in these mantras can get through.

Each mantra will be relevant to a particular stage in the death process. If the deceased has studied and meditated on the Bardo Thodol during his lifetime he will recognize the various stages of the death process as it unfolds. In another sense a dialogue is being set up between the dead or dying person and the living one; the dead are being helped to find their way. The readings will usually be for four hours in the morning, and again in the afternoon. In the Tibetan monasteries there were often very elaborate ceremonies when the abbot died. The readings would go on for the full forty-nine days and Mahakala dances were performed by monks in black robes accompanied by death music on drums, with invocation of the gods of death Mahakala or Yama.

Padma Sambhava gathered together the teachings of the old religion, and produced his book giving it a Buddhist slant. Some three hundred years later the text was further clarified

by Milarepa whose own classic work was known as Kur Bum –
'One hundred thousand Songs'. In one of them the devotee is
admonished thus:

> Learn about the clear light of death;
> Learn about the deceptive forms of the Bardo;
> Learn, so you may incarnate by your own powers.

There are said to be three stages of the death process:
Chikhai, Chonyid and Sidpa. At the moment of physical
death there is a progressive dissolution of the elements of
consciousness. Sight, hearing, smell, taste and touch all
disappear. Then the sense of one's own body disappears, and
whatever seemed to be outside the body now seems to be
inside it. Mental activity ceases, various sounds are heard, and
the clear light appears. The awareness is of a state that is
timeless and boundless, all knowing, and incredibly blissful, a
state akin to samadhi. It is said that the yogi, having
previously attained to the samadhi state and knowing what to
expect, will hold on to the clear light and try to abide in it.
Others will be frightened by its intensity and emptiness, and
move on quickly to the second clear light, dimmer than the
first due to karmic obscuration.

The first clear light is said to average in time 'one meal
period'. So this might be taken as up to one hour. The second
clear light can last from three and a half to four days. After
this the soul no longer stays in the vicinity of the dead body,
and the etheric body dissolves. In Tibetan yoga there are
many meditations on the clear light, and as in yoga the adept
is seeking always to reach the state of samadhi in his
meditations. So samadhi or nirvana is sought for its own sake,
and also as preparation for the onset of the clear light at
death.

The Chikhai, or first period of the death experience
described in the Bardo Thodol, corresponds closely to
accounts given by people who have technically died, but were
brought back to life by resuscitation. They describe the
sounds of dissolution, the experience of going through a
tunnel, and then the clear light. Often they are out of the
body, and afterwards can describe what happened at the

deathbed or scene of the accident. The ghost of the dead person has often been seen for up to four days afterwards.

The soul now enters the second stage, the Chonyid Bardo, and is visited for the next seven days by certain karmic visions. These are karmic residues manifested mostly in exaggerated and symbolic form in the same manner as dreams. For seven days the dreams are of a peaceful nature, and are referred to as the peaceful deities. They are followed during the next seven days by visions of a threatening, fearful and terrifying sort, referred to as the wrathful deities. There are said to be forty-two peaceful and fifty-eight wrathful deities. Although in the Bardo Thodol they are gods and demons, all with their own names, in Jungian psychology they would be recognized as archetypes. At first the happy and pleasant parts of our nature are manifest. Later, as we go deeper, those aspects that are guilt-laden or repressed come into manifestation. The soul remembers, and having no defence against its own memories, no activities or opiates to turn to, is tormented by them.

The peaceful and wrathful deities appear as mandalas. Each of the deities or archetypes has a darker and a brighter aspect shining within the mandala. Both the lights and the mandala change each day. The wrathful deities are stated to be the exact obverse of the peaceful deities. Whereas earlier they were set in beautiful colours now they are flame-enhaloed and blood drinking. In their presence the ordinary mortal will feel fear, terror and awe. The yogi on the other hand will already be familiar with them, having met them in his meditations and dreams, and in their painted likenesses on the tankas. It is stated in the text that the yoga adept can take the Bardo by the forelock, knowing that all these visions are unreal and powerless. Both in this world and in other worlds there is really no Bardo to experience. The yoga adept of high spiritual attainment can obtain an immediate conscious rebirth back into the physical world, or into one of the paradise realms.

The soul now enters the third stage, the Sidpa Bardo. Here it wanders. In the Sidpa Bardo thought is everything. Whatever a soul thinks it happens. Whatever it desires it can have. It can go anywhere it likes in the whole world, and can

visit relatives and friends. Everything is its own mental
projection. It is however impossible for the soul to progress in
the Bardo. Because of this the Bardo Thodol warns against
'calling-up' such spirits. Such calling-up will prolong their
stay in the Bardo by giving them the impression that they are
as real physically as those who have contacted them.

After the wanderings in the Bardo, which can be very long,
up to one thousand years, or take only a few days, the lights of
physical existence appear. They are first very dim, but get
progressively brighter, until the soul feels pulled towards
them, and lands among the shimmering lights at the moment
of birth. It is stated that before rebirth the adept who is free
of all residual karma may choose whether to incarnate at all
on earth, or whether to go to one of the paradise realms that
are now shown to him. If the adept not needing to reincarnate still chooses birth it will be as a teacher of the spiritual
life. He will make his own choice of parents, and of the time,
place and circumstances of his birth. Lesser mortals are more
restricted, but even for them some measure of choice
remains. The 'Lords of Karma' arrange the circumstances of
rebirth, and one is born into circumstances largely pre-
ordained by one's own karmic tendencies.

An old established yoga mental exercise is thinking backwards. The aspirant recalls the events of the day in reverse
order. This is contrary to our natural tendency, which is to
think forward. It can be very difficult to accomplish, but once
mastered the process is taken further – to recollect the events
of the week, then of the year, and next of the life. The recall is
then taken through the birth experience into the pre-birth
state. The yogi also becomes aware of his own mental state
during sleep, and can often go very deeply into the subconscious. In these deep layers of the mind are met the karmic
visions so blissful or terrifying that visit one in the Chonyid
stage of the Bardo.

Between Padma Sambhava's first draft of the Bardo
Thodol and its condensation and clarification by Milarepa a
great deal of experimentation appears to have gone on in
Tibet to prove the truth of these teachings. It was regular
practice for high Lamas of spiritual attainment to 'die' by
suspending the breath and mental activity. Then under strict

supervision by their helpers, who carefully watched over their body, they would bring back their bardo experiences. Since the development of resuscitation techniques in hospitals there have been a growing number of near-death experiences recorded.

It was also common practice for High Lamas to regress into the Sidpa Bardo, and bring back pre-birth memories. Today regression under hypnosis has become fairly common practice, and again the testimony of those regressed agrees in the main with the Bardo Thodol. It is interesting that though many devout Christians have undergone regression or resuscitation none has brought back experiences involving a judgment, which is such an important doctrine in Christian teachings on death and the hereafter. The Bardo Thodol makes no mention of a judgment.

Both the older yoga meditation practices and the modern resuscitation and regression methods have brought forward much information on the Chikhai and Sidpa stages, but neither has helped a great deal with the Chonyid stage of wanderings in the bardo. Spiritualism is the only source of information here. In its literature thousands of cases of contact through mediums have been recorded, many containing corroborative evidence. The fact that most of the messages are trite and inconsequential would seem to confirm the teachings of the Bardo Thodol that souls wandering in the bardo can make no progress, but are merely turning over old memories and relationships. Only when incarnate can a soul make progress.

The whole burden of the Bardo Thodol, apart from making passage through the bardo easier, is to escape rebirth altogether. Life in a physical body is considered to be hard and unwelcome. Much of Indian thought is on this theme. The testimony of those having near-death experiences, or who have been regressed beyond birth say the same thing. Few of those who had died wished to come back to life, and few of those regressed wanted to be born.

Such then is the Tibetan Book of the Dead, a contribution to yoga quite different from anything that had gone before. Its full value will not be assessed for many generations, because mankind does not yet have enough control over the process of death, nor enough control of his environment to ensure that everyone may eventually experience a smooth transition from this world to the next phase of his existence. We have already said that though Padma Sambhava made the first draft of this unique work it was Milarepa nearly three hundred years later who put it into the form we have today.

Milarepa himself has been described as Tibet's greatest yogi. He was the fourth of a succession that began with Tilopa, an Indian yogi of considerable attainment. Tilopa was a tantric. He never left Bengal, yet is revered by all Tibetans as the real founder of the Kargyutpa sect. Tilopa was an advocate of the 'short path' to enlightenment. Many stories are told of his rough manners. The fact that he ate meat and fish, mocked the caste system, indulged in various unseemly activities of the left-hand path, and was extremely cruel to his disciples seemed to have endeared him to the Tibetans, but was shocking to most Indians.

The short path was the same that later became such a feature of Zen. It relies on shock tactics to produce enlightenment. Tilopa's most ardent disciple was Naropa. Many stories are told of the trials and tribulations that Naropa had to undergo at Tilopa's hands. During the many years that Naropa was enduring these ordeals Tilopa taught him nothing of a spiritual nature, yet Naropa was evidently learning the methods of Tilopa. Naropa finally received his enlightenment. One evening they were both seated by a fire in the open when Tilopa suddenly hit Naropa very hard across the cheek. Naropa relates how he 'saw all the stars of heaven', and at the same time the inner meaning of the short path also flashed into his mind.

Naropa began to teach the short path himself, and eventually gained the rather forbidding Tibetan Marpa as a student. Marpa in turn learned the method of the short path; it could not be called a doctrine. He then returned to Tibet. Although his master Naropa was a gentle person who treated his disciples with respect, Marpa outdid even Tilopa in his cruelty. He subjected his favourite pupil Milarepa to the most brutal indignities, testing his endurance to the limit. Milarepa came through it all hardened and tempered to become the great yogi-magician who has become such a legend in Tibet.

The many exploits of Milarepa cannot be detailed here. His biography by his disciple Rechung was translated into English in 1927 by W.Y. Evans Wentz under the title of 'Tibet's Great Yogi Milarepa'. Even after making due allowance for exaggeration the story of Milarepa's life is truly remarkable.

Of the extraordinary powers gained by yogis four are of major importance. These are the attaining of psychic heat, the fairly widespread use of telepathy for sending messages between monasteries, the ability to move at great speed over long distances, and the ability to recall one's dream experiences on waking up. These powers all had practical utility. The practice of Tumo, or psychic heat, was of immense value in the freezing climate of the Tibetan uplands. It gave its practitioners great freedom of movement. The art itself takes three years to master, and consists of a series of extremely complex breathing exercises combined with visualizations and the intoning of mantras. The word repa means cotton-clad, so Milarepa was cotton-clad Mila. The mark of a repa in Tibet is the wearing of only a cotton robe.

Sending messages between monasteries had a very utilitarian purpose in view of the dangers and uncertainties of carrying messages by word of mouth or by hand. At a set time of each day a sender and receiver would sit and write down what was received, or was to be sent. The messages usually informed another monastery of something they needed, or of a visitor who was coming their way, and should be met. The Lung-gom-pas were a class of adept able to travel long distances at about twice the normal speed. Even quite recently travellers have reported seeing them. They are in a state of trance, and some wear heavy chains to keep themselves from leaving the ground. Those who have seen them report that their feet seem hardly to be touching the ground, and they seem to be leaping rather than running. This training too is long and exacting, and again makes use of breathing exercises, visualizations and mantras. The Lung-gom-pa intones a particular mantra all the time he is running.

The fourth of the extraordinary powers really belongs to a totally different genre of practices, but differs from them in having an immediate practical value. The idea of 'sleeping on a problem' is well known. Patanjali in his sutras has pointed out that the disciple may obtain instruction during sleep, and sometimes people will awaken with the memory of a pre-cognitive dream. The Tibetan yogis were familiar with all these aspects of the sleep state, and many more besides. Their long meditations had made them aware of the subtle border-land between sleep and waking consciousness, and of the various layers of sleep. They were able to put themselves in touch with others, and with various events, including the spirit worlds, and recall what they had experienced.

This fourth of the extraordinary powers is included in the 'Six Doctrines' of Naropa and his sister Niguma of the 'Great Symbol' school, which later became known as the Kargyutpa school. Naropa lived from 1016 to 1100. The six doctrines are 'the psychic heat', 'the illusory body', 'the dream state', 'the clear light', 'the intermediate state', and 'the trans-mission of consciousness'. The psychic heat and the dream state have already been discussed. By the illusory body is meant the eventual realization that everything is maya. This idea, first presented in the Upanishads, was restated with greater clarity and elaboration by Sankara. The student was required to have thoroughly studied all these writings to become an initiate of the Great Symbol school.

The last three doctrines are concerned with the teachings embodied in the Bardo Thodol. The doctrine of the clear light describes the methods employed to cause to arise in consciousness, and to become familiar with, the clear light experienced at death. In experiencing the clear light during the day time the student sits for meditation and gets into the right frame of mind by practising the six rules of Tilopa: 'do not imagine, ponder, analyse or concentrate, avoid introspec-tion, stay in the state of nature'. To experience the clear light during the night time he lies on the right side and visualizes a four-petalled lotus flower, then subsides into it. When the visualization can no longer be held he must imagine that it is turning into clear white light. So recognition of the clear light is accomplished between waking and sleeping, at the exact moment that wakefulness becomes sleep. These exercises will prepare him for the clear light of death. At that time the yogi is to hold on to the experience, and abide in the clear light for as long as possible.

Doctrines concerning 'the intermediate state' and 'the transmission of consciousness', are descriptions of the Chonyid bardo, where the soul wanders, and of Sidpa, where the soul seeks rebirth. The student is required to study the extremely complex manifestations and archetypes to be met with in the Chonyid, and to recognize the signs of approaching rebirth in the Sidpa bardo.

The impetus given by Padma Sambhava had largely expended itself when Marpa introduced the 'short path' teaching into Tibet. The uncompromising dedication to yoga of himself and his pupil Milarepa resulted in a kind of golden age which saw the further development of siddhis, and of various meditative aids such as mandalas and yantras – geometrical designs on the floor – again for meditation, but often involving movement and dancing.

Marpa and Milarepa saved a vast number of Buddhist texts from the Moslem invaders who at that time were advancing across north India, and indulging in the age-old ritual of burning the books. Many journeys were made over the frozen wastes of the Himalayas to the university of Nalanda and other centres of learning, collecting the precious documents. Eventually Nalanda was sacked by the invaders, and everything destroyed. But the most valuable writings had been saved, and came to influence Tibetan culture profoundly. The result was that the Tibetan Buddhist canon became the most extensive in all Buddhist literature, comprising one hundred and eight volumes of words of the Buddha, and two hundred and twenty-five tantras. They were finally collected together by Bu-tson in 1290.

In the times of Milarepa the Bonpos clung to the old religion, the Ningmapas were the followers of Padma Sambhava and the Kargyutpas represented the Tilopa, Naropa, Marpa and Milarepa stream. These were now joined by the Gelugpas, an order founded by an Indian monk, Atisha. He brought another brand of tantrism, but more intellectual, and founded a monastic system. A strong esoteric tradition based on succession was, and still is, a feature of this sect.

The Gelugpas became more acceptable to the populace following reforms by Tson-ka-pa (1357-1419), who came from Am-Do in north-west China. Often referred to as the man from the onion land he is more reverently known as Je Rimpoche, or Glorious Chief. His tomb at Ganden is a place of pilgrimage to this day. He eliminated much of the older ritualism and traces of Bon influence, and introduced some elements from Theravada Buddhism. Among these were the Vinaya rules, rules of conduct for monks and laity. His principal work was the Lam Nin Chembo in two parts, one for the priests, the other for the general populace. Other later sects are the Sakhyas, named after the colour of the soil where the sect was established, and the Dugpas. The latter were responsible for some later changes and elucidations of the Bardo Thodol.

The Gelugpas eventually took over from the Kargyutpas as the largest sect. Their Grand Lama, known in Tibet as Kyamgon Rimpoche, is better known to the outside world as the Dalai Lama. The fifth Dalai Lama allied himself with the Chinese emperor during a period of anarchy, and as a result was able to take over the entire country in 1615. Assisted by the Tashi Lama, who had jurisdiction over eastern Tibet he ruled the country until the Chinese invasion in 1968. The monks of the Gelugpa order are distinguished by the wearing of yellow hats, whereas the Kargyutpas and the Ningmapas wear red, and the Bons black.

The Gelugpas have put great emphasis on the doctrine of reincarnation. This has resulted in a wealth of anecdotes and stories of rebirths into higher or lower orders of society depending on the way life was lived in former times. At a more scholarly level there are many erudite works theorizing on the reincarnation mechanism. Any claim to be the reincarnation of some dignitary or famous person is exhaustively investigated, the most exacting of such investigations being when the Dalai Lama himself dies. Within two years of his death a boy child must be found carrying certain distinguishing marks on his body, and be able to pick out objects used by him in his previous life. Some well authenticated accounts of these investigations have been published, including those relating to the present Dalai Lama.

Although Tibet is so remote, its literature is the most extensive and detailed of any in the East, so there is a great treasure-house of material both of a yogic, and of a general cultural nature, yet to be garnered there.

CHAPTER 13
Zen

It has always been customary to refer to the devotee of Zen as a Zen yogi, when he is somewhat advanced along the way. This convention acknowledges the yogic rather than the religious basis of Zen. D.T. Suzuki, the most illustrious of modern commentators on the subject, abides by this convention in his classic three-volume work 'Essays in Zen', and in his other writings.

Zen has been described as an offshoot of the Yogacara school of Indian Buddhism. It is the 'Mind-Only' school, whose central doctrine is that pure consciousness is the ultimate reality. The material world, and the concepts of mind are dependent on the central fact of consciousness, and no longer exist when consciousness is withdrawn. This doctrine puts meditation in a dominant position in religious practice, and in the yogic techniques of self-awareness and the striving for enlightenment.

We have already noted that this school was the parent of tantrism, with its encouragement of intuition, emotion and practical experience. It has declared that intellection does not lead to a knowledge of reality, nor does morality take us much beyond the level of mere social conformity. So any metaphysical or religious principles based only on intellectual concepts or moral behaviour ultimately lead nowhere. To formulate intellectual concepts on the one hand and moral precepts on the other is an exercise involving withdrawal from the running stream of life while the formulation is being made. Then to try to live your life according to these rules encourages this withdrawal: to live a half life. Tantrism brought the emotional element into religious life to enable the average person to live more fully. The intellect and the moral precepts were entirely secondary to living a full life with all its potential, so should also be secondary in any complete religion.

Zen too has always been at pains to insist that it is not only anti-intellectual and anti-morality, but also anti-religious. The writings of its leaders are proof of this. But if neither intellect, morality nor religion find any foothold in it, what is left? The answer is yoga, and a very distinctive brand of it. Technique, method and personal experience are everything in Zen. Tantrism, although introduced into China and Japan in the eighth century AD, never really put down roots in those countries. It was the last arrival from India. The Chinese school was known as Chen-yen Tsung (Japanese Shingon).

The emotional element in Tantrism had no appeal, but the intuitive element in its Yogacara parent did. If the object of all religious endeavour was to experience samadhi and attain to enlightenment about ultimate reality, intuition must be the way to realize it, as the older ways of intellectual speculation on the one hand and mere morality on the other were both discredited. Intuition comes only in flashes. It is not built up gradually over a long period by means of various practices. Therefore a flash of enlightenment can happen at any time. This reasoning led to the development of the Short path, of which Tilopa, the father of the Kargyutpa sect in Tibet was an exponent.

The founder of the Chinese meditation school of the Short path, or enlightenment by sudden intuition, was Boddhid-harma. He came from Conjeeveram in south India, and was the twenty-eighth patriarch, in direct line of succession from Gotama the Buddha himself. When Boddhidharma left India without appointing a successor the line of Indian patriarchs came to an end. He arrived in China in AD 552. Both Theravada and Mahayana Buddhism were already estab-lished there owing to the migration of a constant stream of Indian monks from the time of Emperor Ashoka, and traffic in the opposite direction, in the shape of Chinese pilgrims and scholars visiting Buddhist and Hindu shrines in India. Buddhism had become influential in China in the third century, and increased in power and influence in the fourth, during the time of the Tang dynasty. So Boddhidharma arrived at a time when China was open to all Indian ideas, and had much goodwill towards them.

It has often been asked, 'Why did Boddhidharma leave India for China?' He was head of the Buddhist church, yet he left without appointing a successor. For a clue we should look again at the date, and consider what was happening in India at the time. Buddhism was decadent and in decline. Its compromises with Hinduism were such that the two had become almost indistinguishable. The early message of Gotama was all but lost, and the new stirrings were in the direction of bhakti and tantra, with Mahayana becoming dominant, and disrupting the older Theravada. Boddhidharma had a reputation for fierceness and outspokenness. Perhaps he felt that the trend was running so strongly against his own views that any attempt on his part to redress the balance was doomed to failure. China, on the other hand, was receptive to Indian teachings. Doubtless he had met Chinese pilgrims visiting the Indian shrines. He therefore decided on pastures new. He may also have decided deliberately to cut the line of patriarchs by leaving, in the belief that this line of succession was tending to ossify Buddhism into an institution and power base, rather than a living religion.

Every Zen devotee knows the story of Boddhidharma's arrival in China. He occupied a cave near the imperial city, and there began to teach. In view of his importance as the twenty-eighth patriarch he would have no shortage of students. After some time the emperor Wu came to see him. The emperor asked, 'what is the basic principle of your teaching?' 'Vast emptiness', was the reply, 'and nothing in it that can be called holy.' 'Who are you then?' asked the emperor. 'I do not know', said Boddhidharma. On another occasion the emperor questioned him on the vexed question of the earning of merit. He said, 'I have done a great deal to encourage the spread of Buddhism in China. I have built temples and monasteries, and supported many monks and nuns. I have also had many Buddhist works translated. What merit have I gained from all this?' Boddhidharma's reply was, 'none whatsoever'.

It is evident from these early conversations that Boddhidharma had no use for the usual trappings of religion, and that he was a Mahayanist in basic philosophy. His 'vast emptiness' was the doctrine of sunyata (void). But Boddhidharma seems to have moved even beyond Mahayana, out of the realm of speculation altogether, and into the world of experience, and the techniques to make the enlightenment of samadhi possible. He had moved even closer to the core of yoga with his accent on practical experience, and with a range of techniques to highlight, sharpen and clarify the experience.

During the lifetime of Boddhidharma his became the leading Buddhist school in China. It took the Chinese translation of the Indian word for meditation as its name. The Indian word is dhvana. The Chinese translation is Chan while the Japanese translation is Zen. The yogic self-effort of Chan was to suit the Chinese character better than the rather quietist and moralistic Theravada, and the metaphysical Mahayana schools already established there. Boddhidharma became the first patriarch of the Chan school. He was followed by five others, until the line died out after Hui-Neng (637-713 AD), who left no successor.

The Chan (Zen) school teaches a direct way to enlightenment. It has no formal organization, nor any sacred literature. Although its devotees are encouraged to read sacred literature from any sources and traditions, it is made clear that the reading of literature alone will not lead to enlightenment. At the same time the reading of elevating ideas can create a translucent state of mind which is conducive to the growth of the intuitive faculty, and will better allow the flash of intuition to become manifest when the student is ready. A basic and much quoted saying of Boddhidharma describes both the objective and the method of Zen. This is in the four-line poem:

A special transmission outside the scriptures.
No dependence on words and letters.
Direct pointing to the soul of man.
Seeing into one's own nature.

This is truly a doctrine of no support, which was also claimed for Mahayana. But Zen appears to go even beyond Mahayana, in eschewing even the negative way of understanding things as some support for the mind.

Just as the meeting of Tantrism with Bon produced the extraordinarily rich mixture that we know today as Tibetan

Buddhism, so the meeting of the Chan school with the naturalistic ideas of Taoism modified what originally were purely Indian ideas into the unique body of teaching and technique that has come to be recognized as Zen. There are some who say that Zen is not Buddhist, and never was, and others say that it is more Taoist than Buddhist. The final fusion with Taoist ideals came about under the influence of Hui-Neng, the sixth and last patriarch of the Chan school. With him the last vestige of Indian influence was shed, and Zen in the form we know it today came into being.

The Tao Te Ching is the main scripture of Taoism, and is one of the most sublime pieces of literature of any religious tradition. Along with the Bhagavad Gita and the Bible it can claim to be the most translated and widely read book in the world. It speaks of the Tao as being 'the Way', meaning the path to take, the way to live one's life and the way to understand the workings of natural law. To live by natural law is the way of Tao. To be relaxed and flow with events rather than oppose them, is also the way. The 'Great Tao' also has metaphysical overtones. 'That which has a name is not the eternal Tao'. It also means bending and giving way.

The naturalism of Taoism went well with the anti-intellec-tualism of Zen. They were also at one in considering morality as secondary. Taoism declares that the person living by natural law needs no moral precepts to teach him how to live. It became commonplace for people to become devotees of both cults. There also developed a distinctively Taoist yoga. This was an adaptation of old Taoist ideas to newer yoga practice, and involved the ancient Taoist preoccupation with preserving the body into extreme old age, eventually striving for immortality. This activity had been carried on using various techniques in the past, but after meeting with Zen a technique of meditation was used. A classic work on this meditational technique is 'The Secret of the Golden Flower', translated by Richard Wilhelm. The methods used seem to have been influenced by laya yoga.

The prime source of energy in the body is said to reside at the hara centre – in the pit of the stomach. Energy is stored there, and heat is generated there. Artists' illustrations depict a cauldron of live coals at that point. Universal energy (prana) is drawn in with the breath and stored there. This energy is capable of curing any disease of the body if rightly directed to the weakened part. Chastity is essential to conserve this energy, which must not leak away through sexual activity. Moreover the energy should constantly be drawn upward to the brain to activate the higher centres. If this is done intelligence and insight will increase, and the practitioner will become spiritually awakened. This upward flowing energy is the elixir of life. If it can be kept upward flowing at all times the practitioner will also gain youthful long life.

The upward flowing energy is ultimately used to make for oneself a soul-body. This is formed on the astral plane, and will be waiting as the vehicle to carry the soul through the death experience fully conscious. Thus there will be no break in consciousness between life and death, and the practitioner will retain a full memory of the former earth life. This is all very reminiscent of the Bardo Thodol, and points to a cult of the dead being widespread throughout east Asia.

Flow is a word that sums up Taoism. This concept of flow was responsible for the unique form taken by the martial arts in China and Japan. Judo is entirely Taoist, and is practised on a large scale in the monasteries and zendos (halls for zen training) in Japan. The principle is to give way, and use the strength of your opponent to encompass his defeat. At one time judo and similar martial arts became almost synonymous with Zen.

Immediately following Hui-Neng, and almost contemporary with him, was a further introduction of ideas from the Yogacara school. This provided a considerable fillip for Zen although it was introduced as an entirely separate school. The introduction was made by Hsuan Tsang, the pilgrim and translator. He made a pilgrimage to India, and in the year AD 637 arrived at the university of Nalanda. The principal professor there was Silabadra, aged 106 in that year. He realized that Hsuan Tsang could have an important part to play in the dissemination of Indian ideas in China, and received him warmly. Hsuan Tsang returned to China with a collection of over six hundred Mahayana manuscripts in Sanskrit, and spent the rest of his life translating them into Chinese, with the generous support of the emperor. Zen was considerably enriched by these Mahayana doctrines, and it was largely because of them that it was able to spread so readily into Mongolia, Korea and Japan. Hsuan Tsang's sect was known as Dharmalakshara in China, and Hosso (pure consciousness) in Japan. It became extremely popular, and its popularity coincided with a great influx of Japanese scholars, which considerably influenced the religious thought of that country.

There was a great flowering of Zen genius in the two hundred years after Hui-Neng, and again in the Sung dynasty from 900 to 1,000. There was also schism. In the ninth century Zen split into two schools. These were Lin-chi (Japanese Rinzai) and Tsao Tung (Japanese Soto). Lin-chi developed further the more extreme teachings of Boddhidharma and Hui-Neng, involving sudden enlightenment by shock tactics of one sort or another, while the Tsao Tung preferred a gentler and more gradual approach. The founder of Lin-chi was I Hsuan, commonly known as Rinzai. He outdid Boddhidharma by his forthright remarks, and even poured scorn on the idea of his disciples' wishing to become Boddhisattvas and Buddhas, referring to Gotama as just another bald-headed monk. 'Those who seek enlightenment through him', he said, 'lose all chance of enlightenment.' Another remark was, 'If you encounter Gotama, kill him.' These remarks and many others in similar vein indicate the anti-religious feeling in Zen.

The Rinzai sect was established in Japan in 1191 by the Japanese monk Eisai. The Tsao Tung sect was introduced about a century later by Dogen, sometimes also referred to as Shoyo Daishi, which is a title. In Japan the sect is known as Soto. Dogen held that morality was the first thing to aim at. When human nature had been purified by meditation, self-discipline and the reading of religious writings, we would be ready for the next step, enlightenment. Dogen directed his followers to the practice of the early Buddhist five branches of morality. These were giving alms, gentleness of speech, benevolence in deeds, putting oneself in other people's places, and gratitude. Many Soto Zen followers use idols or pictures of the Buddha, or one of the Boddhisattvas which they worship. Some treat them as gods. This tendency is at the opposite pole to Rinzai Zen, and is ever present in human nature. Whatever religious tradition one looks at the two extremes will be found. Most people seem to need the comfort of worship and prayer, faith in a saviour and a personal God.

In Soto Zen the aspirant sits for meditation (zazen), and eventually finds enlightenment in its practice. The Buddha-nature is to be realized, or recognized, not something to be attained. A key phrase is 'the practice is enlightenment'. No koans are used in Soto Zen, nor is mondo. It is traditional quietist meditation, and marks a return to Indian practice. Soto Zen claims that few people have gained enlightenment by the shock tactics of Rinzai, whereas many thousands have done so through Soto Zen meditation.

The koan as used in Rinzai Zen is a nonsensical statement designed to baffle the intellect, and so render it impotent. As the mind struggles to solve the riddle it is forced into an ever narrower defile until finally it abdicates, and in a flash receives enlightenment. The best-known koan is, 'what is the sound of one hand clapping?' Another is, 'What was your original face before you were born?' Another, a little more abstract is 'All things return to the one. To where does the one return?' There are hundreds of koans, and it appears necessary to find one with an individual appeal in order to produce enlightenment for a particular individual.

Mondo is the other main technique. It comprises a swift exchange of question and answer between master and pupil. The master must be adept at leading the student on, and the student must reply instantly, without pausing for thought. The final result aimed at is the same. The mind abdicates, and the spirit is released into enlightenment.

The koan was a device invented by Daie Soko, born 1089. He advocated it as an alternative to quiet sitting and stilling the mind for those of an intellectual temperament who could not still the mind, and needed to have it occupied doing something. The koan keeps the mind occupied, but not in rational thinking. Its thinking is to no useful end. The Zen yogi knows this, but may find it easier than just sitting. It is freely admitted by most Zen masters that the invention of the koan saved Zen from extinction by way of extreme quietism on the one hand, and by extreme intellectualism on the other.

One or other of these is the fate of any religion once the
original impetus of the founder has spent itself. With the
koan Zen managed to retain the life flow which comes from
self-effort. A Zen master, Chen Ching Ke-wan, has said, 'As
far as Zen is concerned experience is all in all. Anything not
based on experience is outside Zen.' This can also be said of
yoga.

In giving this short history of Zen our claim is that Zen is
entirely yogic, and has been so throughout its history. The
yoga element has been strong in all the schools of Buddhism
in China and Japan. It has also influenced Taoism deeply, and
given it new direction and purpose. Only Confucianism in
China and Shinto in Japan have been unaffected. The reason
is that both are official government ethical systems, which put
their main emphasis on social conformity rather than on
individual freedom, including the ultimate individual freedom, that of samadhi, nirvana or satori as it is referred to in
Japan.

The Yogacara school had a decisive influence on the
development of Zen, as indeed it did on the development of
tantrism throughout India and Tibet. Hatha yoga, which we
consider next, and which developed later than Zen is now
widely practised throughout China and Japan. No Zen
programme is complete without its hatha yoga element.
Whether the devices of mondo and koan will survive is open
to question, but there can be no doubt of the survival of the
more traditional meditation techniques of Soto and the other
Buddhist sects, and of Taoism.

CHAPTER 14
Hatha Yoga

References to asanas (postures and exercises) are found in all yoga literature right back to the Upanishads. At that time the asanas were for purposes of meditation. The body was to be placed in a suitable seated posture so that the aspirant could meditate with a straight spine, and with lungs and stomach not restricted. In such a position the body could be forgotten and rhythmic breathing practised. The classic position has always been Padmasana, or Lotus Seat. In this the legs are crossed, with each foot placed on top of the opposite thigh. The hands are placed on the knees facing upwards, with thumbs and first finger touching. The eyes are focused on the end of the nose, and the tip of the tongue is placed at the roof of the mouth. In this position the body is locked very firmly, so that it is almost impossible to push it over. This position has a quietening effect on the mind and emotions, conducive to meditation, and in this position various pranayamas (breathing exercises) can be undertaken.

Padmasana is really quite an advanced posture. It is best carried through to adult life from childhood. Few adults coming to it for the first time are able to accomplish it without pain. For this reason other seated postures are permissible. When sitting not just for quiet meditation, but for development of siddhis or psychic powers, it was found that some other seated postures were more conducive to such activities. The hands were placed in different ways, from which developed a range of hand gestures known as mudras. The number of breathing exercises increased. A range of cleansing practices came into being known as kriyas, and several body locks known as bandhas, similar to mudras but with a different purpose.

This array of physical practices was considered entirely secondary and subservient to the main practice, which was sitting for meditation with the object of eventually achieving samadhi. These practices were not even mentioned during the classical period, except to say, as in Patanajali and in the Bhagavad Gita that a comfortable seated position was necessary for effective meditation. In the tantric period, however, when attempts were being made to develop the siddhis, more active exercises began to be employed. It was also noticed that the general health of yoga practitioners could often be greatly improved by the practice of certain asanas. It began to be apparent that the purely physical aspect of yoga had its own considerable value.

The Nath yogis of north India took up this aspect of the art, and widened its basis considerably. They flourished from the tenth to the twelfth centuries in the area round Gorakhpur near Nepal. The founder of the Nath yoga sect, also known as Natha-Siddhis, was Goruksanatha or Goruknath. The Gurkhas derive from this area. From all accounts the Nath yogis were extremely vigorous, being devoted to physical fitness. They were much travelled and their way of life was very austere. Being often in situations of great danger they became adept at various martial arts. The fighting traditions of the Gurkhas lend credence to this fact. Claims have also been made that they carried knowledge of these practices into China and were thus instrumental in laying the foundations of the Chinese martial arts such as judo and karate. These claims have not yet been substantiated.

As the Nath yogis were also known as Natha siddhis it is obvious that they were likewise renowned for their psychic powers. They lived quite close to Tibet, at a time when Milarepa had given a further impetus to such experimentation in that country. In pursuance of the siddhis the Natha yogis developed a range of asanas, kriyas, mudras, bandhas and pranayamas. Their yoga became distinguished from the other forms by taking the name hatha yoga. Hatha is a compound word. 'Ha' means sun, and 'tha' means moon. This is a reference to pranayama. The right nostril is positive, and represents the sun. The left is negative, and represents the moon. Both must be brought into balance if our nature is to be balanced. Because, as we saw in laya yoga, the nadis ida, pingala and sushumna form a triple knot at the nose, correct breathing exercises will activate the chakras, and through them the whole internal environment of the body. So although hatha refers only to the breath, hatha yoga has come to mean the whole range of yoga physical exercises.

The Nath yogis were social reformers. They tried to break the caste system, and treated women and outcastes as equals. For their pains they were themselves relegated to a lower caste by the Brahmin establishment. This Natha caste still survives as a very small group living in the Vindhya range of mountains in north India. Today they are largely unaware of the revolution wrought by their forebears. The Nath yogis also attempted to unite Hindus and Buddhists in their region, a fruitless task, but a worthy effort. They appear to have been neither Buddhist nor Hindu themselves; perhaps they were both.

Goruknath and his followers left notes and instructions on the various asanas, mudras, pranayamas, bandhas and kriyas, but not in the form of a complete text. These fragments were gathered together by Svatmarama Swami, also known as Divatma Ram, and published in the fifteenth century as the Hathayogapradipika. It is in the same form as Patanjali's Yoga Sutras, a series of short instructions which require further commentary and elaboration for their elucidation. It is arranged in five sections: 'Initial Practices', 'Stepping up Energy', 'Overcoming Limitations', 'Manifesting Self' and 'Corrective Treatments'.

The first verse states: 'Hatha yoga was given as a ladder, so that he who has the desire may climb to the highest stage of raja yoga.' Although hatha yoga is now practised without reference to the other yogas, such is its popularity, it is evident from this opening that this was never intended. After saluting the great hatha yogis of the Nath tradition and naming twenty-three of them the text goes on to advise on the conditions needed to practise yoga. Yoga is made useless by six things: overeating, exertion, talking, extreme abstinence, public company and unsteadiness of mind. It is achieved by six things: courage, persistence, knowledge, determination and abandonment of public company. The yamas and niyamas (abstinences and observances) of Patanjali's Sutras are then listed.

The first section lists fifteen asanas. These are Svastika, Gomukha, Virasana, Kurmasana, Kukkatasana, Uttanakurasana, Dhanurasana, Matsyendra, Paschimotanasana, Mayurasana, Shavasana, Siddhasana, Padmasana, Dimbhasana and Bhadrasana. These asanas and others can be found illustrated and fully explained in one of the many books now available on the subject.

The second section is concerned with purification and energizing. Specifically this means the practice of pranayama. The object of pranayama is to purify the nadis and build up bio-energy. This leads to the practice of kriya. There are six kriyas: Dhauti, Basti, Neti, Trataka, Nauli and Kapalabhati. Dhauti means to swallow a wet cloth the width of four fingers, and about 24 feet (7 metres) long. The exercise is done gradually, adding an extra metre each day. It has the effect of absorbing catarrh and other impurities in the intestinal tract. Bhasti is done by squatting in a bath of warm water, inserting a rubber tube into the anus, drawing water into the bowel, removing the tube, and then expelling the water. Neti requires the insertion of a soft thread about 9" (23 cm) long up one nostril, and drawing it out through the mouth. Repeat with the other nostril. Trataka means to stare at an object unblinking until the eyes water. Kapalabhati is designed to clear the skull. One breathes in through the nose rapidly, and out again with force. This cleanses the sinus.

In verse forty-three reference is made to the siddhis that may be gained by the above practices. Anima is the ability to move among people without being noticed. Mahima is the opposite ability, to project oneself on other people's attention. Laghima is to become very light, to levitate. Garima is the opposite ability, to remain stationary and motionless against all efforts to move one. This also applies mentally. Prapati is the ability to obtain knowledge of everything. Prakamya is the ability to suspend all physical activity, to remain buried alive for long periods. Vashitwam is the ability to tame wild animals and to control human beings. The eighth and final siddhi is Ishitwam, the ability to animate physical objects, including the recently dead.

The eight kumbhakas or breathing exercises are then explained. They are Surya Bhedana, Ujjiyi, Sitkari, Sitali,

Bhastrika, Bhramari, Murccha, and Plavini. At the end of each session when performing several repetitions of one of the kumbhakas the Jalandhara or Uddiyana Bandha is performed. Verse forty-six states that by synchronizing the contraction of the lower abdomen (Uddiyana Bandha), and the contraction of the throat (Jalandhara Bandha) prana will move through the system. By raising apana upwards, and taking prana downwards, the current of vayu is cleared. The three stages of breath are then explained. They are puraka (inhalation), kumbhaka (retention) and rechaka (exhalation). Time intervals for these are given as 1:4:2. Of these three, kumbhaka is the most important, and during it the mind can be at one or two levels. These are sahita kumbhaka and kevala kumbhaka. At the level of the latter, kundalini may be aroused. This section ends with enumeration of the eight signs of progress. These are slimness of body, clear resonant voice, freedom from disease, bright eyes and lustre of face, control over one's creative energies, good metabolism, purified nadis, total awareness.

The third section gives an explanation of kundalini which has already been dealt with under laya yoga. It then gives instructions on the practice of Kechari or lengthening of the tongue, useful when a yogi decides on hibernation, i.e. being buried alive for a certain period during which breathing and other vital processes are arrested. The lengthened tongue can close the nasal passages from inside the head to prevent leakage in or out of the lungs. It then deals with the three bandhas or locks: uddiyana, mula and jalandhara, and completes this section with an explanation of the ten principal mudras employed in raising kundalini. The ten mudras are Mahamudra, Mahavedha, Kechari, Uddiyana bandha, Mula-bandha, Jalandhara bandha, Viparitakarni, Vajroli, Sahajoli, Amaroli and Shaktichalana.

The fourth section is repetitive and difficult. The title is 'Manifesting Self', and the sub-title is 'Signs of Samadhi'. It opens by referring to nada (sound), bindu (light), kala (change), and proceeds to explain samadhi. Samadhi is a state where energy is no longer manifest and a state of equilibrium is attained. There is no separation of Jivatman (individual self), and Paratman (cosmic self). Only a guru who has himself attained samadhi can tell of it. Indifference to worldly pleasures is necessary to achieve samadhi. Kundalini is raised as a result of performing the various asanas, kumbakhas and mudras. If body and mind have been carefully prepared kundalini will greatly energize the body. In verse eleven it is stated that the yogi who has unleashed the great force of kundalini in himself, yet performs no actions, attains his natural unconditioned state, and when samadhi is attained the yogi is no longer bound by karma. He attains to transcendental knowledge. An exercise to achieve samadhi is to concentrate on the centre of the brain, that part known as the third ventricle. This results in lightness and freedom from tension.

There are seventy-two thousand nadis in the body, but only three of them, ida, pingala and sushumna are made use of in yoga. Unless kundalini can rise without encountering blocks on the way great unease may result. The activity of mind (chitta) is caused by desire (vasana) and by bio-energy (pavana). If one ceases to act, all of them cease to act. Keeping all three in proper balance is the aim of the preliminary stages of yoga. Verse twenty-nine gives the five levels of the mind. They are the senses (indriyas), thinking (manas), the forty-nine psychic energies (maruts), absorption (laya), and cosmic vibration (nada). Verse thirty-two states that laya is an indescribably blissful state but is still not samadhi or moksha.

The forty-nine pyschic energies must be redirected in imagination from the left and right nadis, pingala and ida, into the central nadi sushumna. The activity of the mind then ceases, although energy continues to rise. There must be constant practice of vayu, directing of bio-energies through the margas, the pathways of the body in order to charge up the whole body with pranic energy. This activity must be done daily. The body will then become strong and powerful.

The process of Nadanusandharam is next described. The yogi sits in Muktasana and adopts the pose of the Sahmbhavi mudra. He can then listen to the internal sounds of the body by closing the eyes, using the fingers of both hands to close the nostrils and ears, and performing the throat lock, Jalandhara Bandha. Verse sixty-nine states the four stages of yoga practice. These are Arambha (beginning), Ghata (enthusiastic activity), Parichaya (practical knowledge) and Nishpatti (effortless mastery). These stages are elaborated in the verses that follow. Each of the various stages is accompanied by inner sounds which can be heard by the practice of Shambhavi mudra. The sounds change as the practitioner progresses. At first they are loud and staccato in tone. They become progressively more subtle and musical as progress is made. By concentrating the attention on these internal sounds meditation is made easy, the mind is able to concentrate without too much effort, accumulated personality problems begin to dissolve, and the yogi reaches samadhi. When finally established in samadhi no further sounds are heard. All states of consciousness are transcended and no external stimuli are noticed. The yogi appears as one dead, but is really in a transcendental state of awareness of everything.

Chapter five is headed 'Corrective Treatments' and shows that yoga had linked with Ayurvedic medicine at the time the Hathayogapradipika was written. This section opens with the observation that most people taking up hatha yoga for the first time practise it incorrectly, and so produce various disharmonies, some of which are made manifest in serious ill-health. The practitioner must start again and accept much slower progress. The increase of bio-energy as a result of the exercises is causing these disharmonies. This energy collects at certain points of blockage. Until these blocks are cleared the energy will not run smoothly.

There are three regions of the body: the vata processes operate from the navel to the soles of the feet; pitta processes operate from the navel to the heart; and kapha processes operate above the heart. This description is Ayurvedic. The first thing to do when ill-health occurs is to massage the body with oil, and to follow with hot baths. This is followed by directing prana to the affected part. One should concentrate deeply on the area concerned, and imagine that it is being charged with the energy of prana. Repeated inhalations and exhalations should be performed in order to tone up the lungs and rib cage and to purify the blood. This may be followed by lengthy retention of the breath two or three times. When a condition still persists, shaking of the limbs or the whole body should be resorted to. This can include whirling while standing, and rolling backwards and forwards after making oneself tight like a ball. All these exercises should be followed by deep relaxation in the savasana or corpse position.

The book ends by pointing out that only a combination of yogic and medical methods can cure disease in most cases. Yoga will put right most cases of mild unease before it develops into disease. Medical methods should be used in chronic cases only.

The teachings the of Pradipika were expanded and became more specific in the Hatha yoga classics that followed. These came in fairly quick succession. They were Yoga Pradipa, Vishvakasha, and Anubhava Prakasha. Later came the Yoga-Vajnavalkya, Yogachudamani-Upanishad and the Geranda Samita. Later still, in the seventeenth century, came the Siva Samita. Most of these are merely of historical interest, being fanciful, or making extravagant claims. But the Geranda Samita was outstanding, complementing and completing the work of the Pradipika.

The Geranda Samita is in seven sections. They are 'The Four Internal Dhautis', Asanas, Mudras, Pratyahara, Pranayama, Dhyana, and Samadhi. The work is more articulate than the Pradipika. It is clearer in its expositions. It also includes more material, although it is no longer than the Pradipika, which was very repetitious. The Geranda Samita is more scientific in tone, not making too many extravagant claims. It is in the form of an explanation by the master Geranda to one of his students.

Like the Pradipika before it, the Geranda Samita opens with the reminder that hatha yoga is a ladder whereby those who will can climb to the highest state of raja yoga. First it lists the shatkarmas or six basic kriyas – cleansing exercises. These are Dhauti (cleaning the teeth, mouth and alimentary canal); Vasti (cleaning out the bowels); Neti (cleaning of the nostrils); Laulika (toning of the abdominal muscles); Traraka (improving the condition of the eyes); and finally Kapalabhati (cleansing the sinuses). There are four internal dhautis, known as antardhautis. The first is drinking air into the mouth as one would drink water. In this way the stomach and intestines are gradually filled with air which is then expelled via the rectum. The second is to do the same with water. The third dhauti is Ujjai, or pressing the stomach wall back against the spine. The fourth internal dhauti is washing the intestines by drawing them out of the body while standing in water; a practice which is quite impossible.

Dantadhauti consists of cleaning the teeth, the root of the tongue, the eustachian tubes of the ear and the frontal sinuses. The second dantadhauti is rubbing the depression in the forehead above the bridge of the nose with the thumb. This helps to clear the head. Hrddhauti gives three ways of cleansing the throat. These are inserting a pliable cane to draw out bile and phlegm. The second is by vomiting. The third, vaso-dhauti, is swallowing a muslin cloth the width of four fingers, then pulling it out again. The final dhauti is Mula-sodhana: cleaning the rectum by inserting the middle finger.

Vasti is alternately contracting and dilating the anal sphincter muscle. In neti-kriya a cotton thread is inserted into one nostril to come out into the mouth. It is then worked backwards and forwards. The other nostril is treated in the same way. Laulika comprises moving the stomach violently from side to side. Trataka is gazing at an object without blinking until tears begin to flow. Kapalabhati is of three kinds: alternate nostril breathing, drawing water through the nostrils and expelling it through the mouth, and drawing water through the mouth and expelling it through the nostrils. These are the kriyas listed in part one. Most are easy to do and are useful, some are difficult, some are impossible.

The second part of the Geranda Samita deals with asanas, and lists thirty-two. They are Siddha, Padma, Bhadra, Mukta, Vajra, Svastika, Simmha, Gomukha, Vira, Dhanus, Savasana, Gupta, Matsya, Matsyendra, Goraksa, Pascimottana, Utkata, Samkata, Mayura, Kukkuta, Kurma, Uttana Kurmaka, Uttana Manduka, Vrksa, Manduka, Garuda, Vrsa, Salabha, Makara, Ustra, Bhujanga, and finally Yoga Mudra. Instructions are given for the practice of each one.

The third part is on mudras. The mudras are rarely practised in the West. Twenty-five are listed. They are Maha-mudra, Nabho-mudra, Uddhiyana, Jalandhara, Mulabhanda,

Mahabandha, Mahavedha, Kechari, Viparitakarani, Yoni, Vajroli, Sakticalana, Tadagi, Manduki, Sambhavi, Partivi, Ambhasi, Agneyi, Vayavi, Akasi Dharana, Aswini, Pasini, Kaki, Natangi and Bhujangini. This is the longest section of the book, and represents an important contribution to hatha yoga.

The fourth part deals briefly with pratyahara – detaching the mind from sense objects. The fifth part is on pranayama. It begins by listing four things necessary to its practice. They are a good place, the right time, moderate food and purification of the nadis. Much is said about the right kinds of food. The nadis are cleansed by alternate nostril breathing, keeping the intervals exact and rhythmic. At the same time one visualizes each chakra in turn, and intones its mantra. Then follows an explanation of the eight basic pranayamas already listed in the Hathayogapradipika. Parts six and seven touch briefly on dhyana and samadhi respectively. They suggest as meditative aids the visualization of beautiful scenes in the case of dhyana, and contemplation of God within in the case of samadhi.

It can truly be said that hatha yoga has extended the practice of yoga into the medical field. The influence of the Tridosha theory of Ayurvedic medicine can be seen in the classics, starting with the Pradipika. Many early practitioners were Ayurvedic physicians. Yoga therapy, of which much is spoken today, really began with hatha yoga. At the time of Goraknath, Ayurveda was well established, and much more advanced than European medicine. It had a large battery of medicines, mostly herbs, surgery and anaesthetics, and a system of diagnosis involving typing of humanity using astrological and physiological indications. It became common practice for Ayurvedic physicians to use hatha yoga as a system of preventive medicine, while they concentrated on chronic conditions. This is still the case today, and will surely become the norm in Western medicine also in due course.

It is now obvious that the movement started by the Nath yogis has gained a lot of momentum, and is very much a force to be reckoned with. As hatha yoga faces the challenge of the findings of biological science and the alternative therapies, it will inevitably change. Some of the exaggerated claims made for it in the past and even today will be moderated in the light of critical scientific investigation. It may well move forward by absorbing most of the alternative therapies into itself. It is the natural leader, being the only discipline having a broad philosophical, not to say spiritual basis, laid down earlier by all the other yogas.

CHAPTER 15
Yoga Moves Westward

The movement of yoga westwards came first of all via the Sufis. They were, and still are, freethinking mystics within Islam. When the Moslem invasions of India occurred between 1200 and 1700 the Sufis, who followed the more aggressive and zealous factions, began to come into close contact with all aspects of Indian religious life. Many of them joined in attempts to unite Hinduism and Islam, but only one of these attempts was at all successful. This was Sikhism, founded by Guru Nanak who was born in 1469.

Sufism first came into prominence in the Umayyad period (661-749). It was characterized by asceticism, mysticism and intuitive knowledge. The Sufis claimed to have inner knowledge of God (kashf), which they considered to be superior to traditional prophetic knowledge (wahy). Kashf is beyond and inaccessible to intellectual knowledge. The striking similarity of these ideas with yoga lends credence to the theory that there was regular contact between the Sufis and Indian mystics of various persuasions. Certainly there has always been much commerce and cultural exchange between India and the countries of the fertile crescent in the eastern Mediterranean.

Before the Moslem invasions of India Islam had established itself in Iran by completely destroying the indigenous religion of Zoroastrianism. A remnant of adherents fled to India, and were allowed to settle in Bombay on condition that they did not proselytize. These were the Parsees, who still remain as a small close-knit community there. Though nominally now Moslem, the influence of the old religion remained strong and the Iranians began to develop their own distinctive brand of Islam, helped in this by the proximity of India. Iran means aryan, and refers to the same aryans who invaded India. The Persian language is very close to Urdu, Punjabi and other languages of north India. In view of these connections it was inevitable that Indian religious ideas had considerable influence. Mysticism cannot flourish naturally under an authoritative religion such as Islam, but the Sufis have managed to become influential by thinly disguising their philosophy as poetry. The Persian mystics such as Halevy, Omar Khayyam and Jalaludin Rumi – founder of the whirling dervishes – carried on a fine tradition of mystical poetry which is still read today. A contemporary Sufi poet with a worldwide readership is Kahlil Gibran.

Over the years the Sufis have grown in importance in Islam, and their influence is particularly strong today in Syria, Lebanon and Turkey, as well as in Iran and India. They have developed some very distinctive forms of meditation, and other popular practices such as chanting in unison, movement and dancing, and the reading aloud of poetry and Sufi stories. These moral tales are instructive, and often very amusing. Many modern Sufis refer to their distinctive practices as Sufi yoga. If we can allow that there is such a thing we could say that its most distinctive feature is its humour. Yoga has not been marked hitherto by much display of humour, so the Sufi contribution is very welcome.

One of India's most eminent free-thinking mystics was Kabir (1435-1518). An illegitimate weaver, he came into contact with the Sufis and regarded himself as one of them, though he was not a Moslem. Neither was he a Hindu, though he believed in reincarnation and karma, and also in the doctrine of maya. He was contemptuous of all religious forms, and considered himself to be a jivanmukti, and therefore beyond them. Kabir had taken initiation from Ramanand, a leading bhakti mystic who advocated a fusion between Islam and Hinduism. Such fusion attempts were being made continually in different parts of India. Goraknath attempted it, as we have seen. The bhakti movement is considered to have ended at the time of Kabir. The book 'Goraknath-ki-Ghosthi' is a controversial dialogue between Kabir and Goraknath regarding their respective doctrines. As Goraknath lived some time before Kabir the author has taken some historical licence, but the book is of interest in giving Kabir's views on hatha yoga, of which he did not approve. He felt that this new development was taking yoga away from its spiritual roots. Kabir is important for his influence on Guru Nanak, for his fondness for the Sufis, and for his independence of both Hinduism and Islam.

The four stages on the path of Sufism show strong similarities with yoga. They are: hast (religious observance); taregut (meditation); araff (development of psychic powers); and hagegut (attainment of sainthood). But the most disturbing influence from the point of view of the orthodox Moslems was that of monism, the doctrine of Advaita Vedanta. Jalaludin Rumi (1207-73) in his long didactic poem, 'Masnavi', advocated a monism almost identical with that of Sankara. Ibn-al-Arabi, who died in 1240, was entirely monist. Sufi poetry has been full of it ever since. Mystical union is their constant theme. Most Islamic missionary effort has been by Sufis, and undoubtedly their embracing of monism has helped them to attract converts among educated Indians. They do a great deal of educational work.

Relations between Sufis and orthodoxy have always been tense, causing them to be forever defending themselves and their doctrines. But the Sufis appear to be gaining the ascendancy. Not least of the practices that cause the orthodox some distress is the Sufi preoccupation with gaining psychic powers. This has taken the form of providing food and other help for their disciples by apports, and also the practice of bilocation. To develop these occult powers the Sufis resort to 'Sama', working themselves up into a trance state by music and dancing. Conspicuous among these are the whirling dervishes. Many of the psychics are women, a strange situation considering the subjection of women in Islam. Sufi ascetics have three watchwords: 'little sleep, little talk, little food'.

The yoga influence that percolated westwards via the Sufis never reached Europe. When it did come its influence was felt first of all in Britain, by way of returning colonial administrators, soldiers, travellers and scholars. Indian philosophy began to be studied in the universities of Europe as early as the eighteenth century, mainly associated with study of the indo-aryan group of languages. The German philosopher, Schopenhauer (1788-1860), was the first to go on record in praise of Indian philosophy. He was so astonished on reading the Upanishads for the first time that he exclaimed: 'Compared to these ancient rishis we philosophers in the west are still in the kindergarten.' The German philosopher, Schlegal, learned Sanskrit from Alexander Hamilton who spoke on yoga in Scotland in 1814, and Paul Deussen (1845-1919) also took up the study of Indian philosophy.

Interest mushroomed, and many scholars studied Sanskrit, and began to translate the Indian classics. One of the best known was Max Muller who translated the Upanishads and the Vedas. Sir John Woodroffe (who also used the pen name of Arthur Avalon), a high court judge in Calcutta, translated some of the tantras. Professor and Mrs Rhys Davids translated the Theravada scriptures, and W.Y. Evans-Wentz some of the Tibetan classics.

British army officers and civil servants came to have great respect for Indian attitudes to life. Their non-violence in the face of extreme provocation was particularly impressive. Some of the famous siddha yogis became known to the new rulers for their extraordinary powers, and were befriended by them. Many visited Europe. The first, in 1830, was Ram Mohan Roy, a great social reformer, and one of the founders of modern India. Keshab Chandra Sen, a devotee of Ramakrishna was received by Queen Victoria, and addressed huge audiences in Britain. Queen Victoria also received Govindananda Bharati (1826-1963) no fewer than eighteen times. The life span of Govinda, one hundred and thirty-seven years, is a striking example of the benefits of the yoga way of life.

One of the most important influences in the spread of yoga to the West has been the Ramakrishna Mission. Ramakrishna (1836-86) was born in Calcutta, a brahmin. At the age of seven he became god-intoxicated, repeatedly falling into trance and spending most of the time in a high state of ecstasy. He took up priestly duties at a temple in Calcutta devoted to the worship of Kali. He wanted only to immerse himself in Kali as the female personification of god. Such was his religious devotion that he neglected his priestly duties, and had to leave the temple. His moods alternated between ecstasy and despair. He was married at the age of twenty-three, but never consummated it. All his life he fought against sexual feelings and against money. Towards the end of his life he was unable to handle any coinage. A story is told of a disciple who put a coin under his mattress. As soon as Ramakrishna lay down on the mattress he leapt up again as though stung by the coin.

On being forced to leave the temple, Ramakrishna took to the forest and became an ascetic. He was joined by a nun, Yogeshwari, who taught him yoga and tantric philosophy. The emotional element in tantra, and the figure of the mother goddess suited his temperament, and his teachings became both yogic and tantric thereafter. Another guru was Totapuri, who taught him Advaita Vedanta. From 1866 Ramakrishna began to study other religions. First he studied Islam, and became a fervent Moslem, observing all its rules and practices, and claimed to have seen a vision of Mahomet. He rejected caste and all social divisions. His talks became famous, and thousands attended them.

He then began to study Christianity, and received instruction from several Christian missionaries. He became a fervent Christian, claiming to have seen Jesus. At one time he actually bore the stigmata on his hands. He wanted to realize the true spirit of Christianity and Islam in his own person, and thus discover for himself the essential unity of all faiths. He never wrote anything, being illiterate, but his talks were collected and published in several volumes. He died at the age of forty-nine with cancer of the throat. No doubt his ascetic practices on top of his epilepsy contributed to his early death.

In 1893 his leading disciple Vivekananda attended the World Parliament of Religions in Chicago. This was followed by tours round America, where he lectured to huge audiences. In the same year he founded the Vedanta Society of New York, followed by others in the major cities. In 1895 he visited Britain, and again attracted large audiences for his lectures on Vedanta and the unity of all faiths. He returned to India in 1897 to found the Ramakrishna Mission, which now has centres throughout the world, and does much educational and philanthropic work in India.

Another Indian destined to have considerable influence worldwide was Aurobindo (1872-1950). He was born in Calcutta, and educated at a Christian convent in Darjeeling.

He continued his education at Manchester Grammer School and Cambridge University where he studied languages. He returned to India where he became an administrator, and was active in the Free India movement. For this he was imprisoned in 1908. In 1910 he went to Pondicherry, then a French colonial enclave in India, to escape the British. There he began to study Sanskrit, and to practise yoga. He founded an ashram which has grown enormously, and completely dominates the town. Later a very ambitious new settlement was established a short distance away known as Auroville.

He referred to his basic philosophy as Integral Yoga. He claimed that it included all the yogas that had gone before, and now prepares mankind for the next great step forward. This is to usher in a transcendental spiritual age, with the divinization of the whole of humanity. The process of this spiritual evolution was for all to reach enlightenment by the practice of yoga. By such practice we reach up to Brahman. Such is the nature of Brahman that when we reach up, Brahman reaches down – a process of grace, rather like the Christian concept. When the two forces meet the gnostic man is created. This is the man of the future. There are now Aurobindo centres all over the world. He too has made a unique contribution to yoga in emphasizing the idea of divine grace, and also in giving a vision of the future which all can identify with.

In 1875 the Theosophical Society was formed in New York by Helena Petrova Blavatsky, a Russian medium, and Henry Steel Olcott, an American. Madame Blavatsky is said to have studied in Tibet for three years to prepare her to bring to Europe and America some of the teachings contained in the very extensive Tibetan canon. Her books, 'Isis Unveiled' and 'The Secret Doctrine', created much controversy, which increased with publication of the 'Mahatma Letters', said to have been apported by various Tibetan masters. It is certainly a fact that most of the knowledge contained in her books was unknown to the West, though none of it would come as a great revelation to someone deeply studied in the Indian classics, particularly the Puranas. The range and depth of knowledge contained in Blavatsky's books is astonishing. Much of it has been corroborated by later research. Although its membership is small, the Theosophical Society has been a catalyst in assisting the acceptance of yogic and occult knowledge in the West. Many other societies and movements have flowed from it. Not least of its valuable activities has been the publication of many hitherto untranslated works of Indian and occult origin.

To add to the Western interest in Indian ideas and practice was the personality and example of Ramana Maharshi (1879-1950). He never left India, but had a pervasive influence with his doctrine of 'vicara' (self-questioning). He was born at Madurai in south India, and at the age of seventeen had a spiritual awakening. This took the form of a great fear of death. He lay on his bed in terror, and imagined that he was already a corpse. He kept asking himself, 'what am I, am I my mind, am I my body, am I my senses?', and so on until nothing remained. But at his last extremity he suddenly realized samadhi.

He immediately left home and all his possessions, and became a hermit and ascetic on Mount Arunachala near by. The ashram which he eventually established at its foot became a place of pilgrimage for thousands. He sometimes lived almost continuously for quite long periods in a state of samadhi, and often switched into trance even while walking. He declared himself to be a strict Advaita Vedantist, and began to teach his simple technique of vicara. He considered that the practice of bhakti and vicara were enough for liberation.

His vicara technique was simply to make people ask themselves 'who am I?' Towards the end of his life he taught only by silence – by direct transmission of the spirit (dakshina-murthi). The transmission was effected by his gaze, which devotees have described as extremely penetrating and compassionate at the same time. He communicated with his helpers by written notes. Many people came to the ashram, and still do so to immerse themselves in its incredibly peaceful atmosphere.

Another yogi who had a considerable impact, especially in America, was Paramahamsa Yogananda (1893-1952). He was ordered by his guru, Sri Yukteswar, to take the yoga teachings to America where he went in 1922, settling in California. He stayed there until his death. Although his life was full of remarkable psychic happenings of many kinds his death was even more remarkable. He died on 7 March 1952 and lay until 27 March when the coffin was finally sealed. During that time no odour of decay was evident, and no change could be seen in his physical condition.

Yogananda's book 'Autobiography of a Yogi' has had a considerable influence, and is a classic of yoga literature. The Self Realization Fellowship which he founded has a world-wide membership running into thousands. When he died he left behind about 160 people at his ashram in Los Angeles. People still come for training to the ashram in great numbers. Yogananda's teaching was straightforward Advaita Vedanta.

In the 1930s a torrent of traveller's tales flooded the market, all testifying to the remarkable feats of Indian yogis. Paul Brunton was a great popularizer, while books by Alexandra David-Neel, who wrote on Tibet, are still in demand. Theos Bernard wrote the first illustrated work on hatha yoga in English, and this started an avalanche of books on the same theme which continues unabated to this day. Sir Paul Dukes, an eminent ex-India civil servant, demonstrated hatha yoga on television in 1949, and started his own school at Epping in Essex.

In the 1970s hundreds of yoga clubs started up throughout Britain. Most were evening classes run by local authorities, but there were also many private classes and clubs. Popular interest received a great boost when Richard Hittlemen and his two attractive female demonstrators began their colour television series in 1973. In 1972 the European Union of National Federations of Yoga was established in Switzerland. Week-long seminars are held annually at the ski resort of Zinal. National bodies are affiliated from all countries in Western Europe, and some from the Eastern bloc are in communication. A 'Minimum Programme' was drawn up, the object being to provide a minimum statement of principles on which all member countries could base their teacher training programmes. It is based on Patanjali's eight limbs of yoga.

At the present time Britain, Europe, North America and Australia have become very familiar with visiting gurus, who usually come like migrant birds in the summer, returning home in the winter. Their disciples meanwhile run their own programmes and maintain a headquarters building.

Swami Sivananda of Rishikesh was responsible for much of this missionary effort. He trained many outstanding yogis at his ashram near Dehra Dun in the Himalayas, and directed them to take the yoga message beyond the shores of India. Among many of them who have made outstanding contributions to the West's understanding of yoga are Swamis Venkatasananda, Satyananda, Satyam, Chidananda and Radha. They all have ashrams in the USA and are regular visitors to Europe and the countries of the English-speaking world.

Sivananda's teaching was basically synthesis. He taught his disciples to accept and practise all the yogas. Due to individual temperament one of them will be central to a person, but efforts should be made to understand and practise the others also. Sankara's Advaita Vedanta was central to his philosophy. Sivananda never left India , but his influence is worldwide. His dedication to Vedanta yoga in the pure Advaita form bequeathed to humanity by Sankara-charya was complete and uncompromising. He was totally opposed to tantra. His ashram was a powerhouse of yoga teaching, and he was himself a very powerful man. Shortly before his death he was quoted as saying, 'I have sown my seed all over the world. It will sprout at the right time.'

Of the many teachers from Sivananda's ashram known to the West, Swami Devananda has been the most active. He went to San Francisco in 1957, and there began to teach. Since then he has established forty Sivananda Yoga Centres and five ashrams, the main one being at Balmoral in Canada. His one- and two-week seminars at the ashram in the Bahamas are extremely popular. Similar seminars are held at the ashram in Canada in the summer.

Devananda like his master is an uncompromising Advaita Vedantist. He is opposed to tantra, and also to some of his illustrious contemporaries, including Rajneesh for encouraging too much freedom, the Maharishi for his levitation techniques, and Sai Baba for his miracles.

Sai Baba is frowned on by many other yogis for his materializations and apports. The classic texts condemn public display of the siddhis, but Sai Baba declares that time is short as we enter a new age, and the spiritualization of humanity must be speeded up. He assists the process by commanding the attention of the common people with his miracles, and points out that Jesus did the same. The gifts that are showered on him are used to build hospitals, schools and orphanages, and he directs a vast organization responsible for this work. His ashram in Bangalore is a place of pilgrimage for thousands, who can be found there every day. His lifestyle is extremely simple. He owns nothing, and accepts nothing for himself. His basic message is also of the simplest: 'Love God, and serve your fellow men with a pure heart.' He gives private audiences, mantras and meditations, and has been responsible for thousands of cures – by touch, command or by absent healing during sleep.

Swami Muktananda is a siddhi yogi with a worldwide following. He has established over 350 Siddha Yoga Centres in 52 countries, 200 of them and 5 ashrams being in the USA. He insists on the traditional guru-chela relationship, and refers often to his own guru, Nityananda. He maintains that power is transmitted along the guru-chela line, and not just teachings.

Muktananda is outstanding for his personal dynamism. He is a first-class businessman who organizes his famous two-day intensives himself, even the travel arrangements. He possesses an overplus of physical and psychic energy, and claims to be able to raise kundalini and other siddhis in his disciples by touch and mantra. Muktananda traces the lineage of his gurus to Kashmiri Shaivism. His intensives take their name from one of their scriptures, the Pratyabhijnahrydam (The Secret of Self Recognition). It consists of twenty short aphorisms which provide a complete map of the processes of creation, limitation and liberation.

The guru with the greatest following in the West until he fell foul of the law is Bhagwan Shree Rajneesh. There are Rajneesh centres throughout the world. Until his move to the USA, as many as 40,000 people visited his ashram at Poona every year. Rajneesh puts his main emphasis on the freedom of the individual. Individual freedom is sacred, and anything that tries to restrict it is to be condemned. He taught open-hearted love to all, and the development of total awareness.

At the many Rajneesh centres there are continuous therapy programmes involving all the natural therapies and sessions in which his devotees let themselves go en masse, with much laughter, embracing and dancing. Total relaxation is the aim. Rajneesh taught what he called dynamic or chaotic meditation. This consists of ten minutes fast breathing, ten minutes of catharsis when one can weep, scream, shake or otherwise let go, ten minutes of shouting the Sufi mantra, 'Hoo', and ten minutes of freezing on the spot without moving. These dynamic meditations are very Sufi in content.

Rajneesh particularly enjoyed studying the various religious traditions, and was refreshingly irreverent about any that have too much head and not enough heart. His discourses were recorded, and appear in book form, which enjoy a wide circulation. A considerable expansion programme has established more ashrams.

The Maharishi hit the world headlines with his system of mantra yoga, to which he gave the name Transcendental Meditation, when the practice was taken up by the British pop stars, the Beatles, in 1967. It has been successful in helping thousands, if not millions of people to overcome stress, and reach a state of tranquillity and integration hitherto denied them. The technique has been so successful that it has been taken up officially by several states in America, by education authorities, public utilities and the private industry.

Its effectiveness lies in its simplicity. A mantra rests the mind from its unceasing activity. Sleep does not fully rest the mind, it recharges the physical body. In TM the rest that the mind receives is of a most remarkable quality. Experiments have shown that the metabolic rate falls below the level of sleep. The heartbeat slows down, but at the same time the flow of oxygen increases, while brainwave patterns show a simultaneous effect of deep relaxation with high alertness.

The Maharishi claims that at the deepest point of meditation the mind is aware of the spaceless, timeless void of its inner being. A feeling of bliss and great tranquillity overwhelms the meditator, and a state akin to that of samadhi is realized. An attempt should be made by the meditator to return to this state twice a day. Two twenty-minute meditation periods must be set aside each day. At these times the meditator merely sits and watches the activity of the mind. After some time the mantra he has received will rise into consciousness. Without making too much effort the mantra should then be repeated for as long as it can be held in mind. As soon as it is replaced with other thoughts the meditation is at an end.

The aspirant pays a great deal of money for a mantra, which is a single word or phrase in Sanskrit taken from an ancient stock. It is selected to suit the uniqueness of each individual, and has no particular meaning. It is given during a short initiation ceremony, and the meditator must return for instruction each day for four days. Although many people are put off by the big business image of the TM movement, the effectiveness of mantra yoga is now plain for all to see.

Yoga is now known to many people throughout the world. For most it is a set of exercises and a way to keep fit. For many others it is a means of training and disciplining the mind. For a growing minority it is thorough-going integral yoga embracing all aspects of human life. Its Indian exponents are still the leaders. Their lives, teachings and exploits are known to millions, and they are looked up to as gurus by countless devotees.

Yoga is also taken seriously by modern science. Hatha yoga is being treated as a therapy in its own right, while researches into physical and mental activity during meditation have resulted in the development of bio-feedback therapy. This therapy is of great value in the treatment of mentally and emotionally disturbed patients. Yoga faces the challenge of scientific research into its claims with every confidence. Both will be enriched by the exercise.

Each age and culture has its own particular emphasis, and our own is no exception. The perspective of yoga is wider than any of them, and is able to transcend any of the blocks or limitations that may be put in its way. In the past it has operated mainly in a religious context. Today it is being called upon to operate in a more scientific and ideological context. It remains as always a free-thinking experimental and experiential discipline requiring self-effort, compassion and knowledge. It has been said that eventually all the religions of the world will be united in yoga. Perhaps they will, for whatever benefits to mind and body may be sought and won on the way the true meaning and sublime object of yoga is union with the Supreme Spirit.

BIBLIOGRAPHY

Asrani, U.A.,'Yoga Unveiled', Dehli, Motilal Banarsidas, 1977.

Blofield, J. 'The Way of Power', London, Allen & Unwin, 1970.

Blofield, J. 'Compassion Yoga', Vermont, Mandala Books, 1977.

Chatterji, M.M., 'Viveka Chudamani', London, Theosophical Publishing House, 1947.

Conze, E., 'Buddhist Scriptures', London, Penguin Books, 1971.

Da Liu, 'The Tao of Health and Longevity', London, Routledge & Kegan Paul, 1980.

David-Neel, A., 'Mystics and Magicians in Tibet', London, Abacus Books, 1977.

Eliade, M., 'Yoga, Immortality and Freedom', London, ARKANA, 1989.

Evans-Wentz, W.Y., 'Tibetan Yoga and Secret Doctrines', Oxford University Press, 1980.

Evans-Wentz, W.Y., 'The Tibetan Book of the Dead', Oxford University Press, 1969.

Evans-Wentz, W.Y., 'Tibet's Great Yogi Milarepa', Oxford University Press, 1974.

Feuerstein, G., 'The Philosophy of Classical Yoga', Manchester University Press, 1980.

Goswami, S.S., 'Laya Yoga', London and Boston, Routledge & Kegan Paul, 1980.

Humphreys, C., 'Buddhism', London, Penguin Books, 1951.

Humphreys, C., 'Zen: A Way of Life', London, Penguin Books, 1962.

Iyengar, B.K.S., 'Light on Yoga', London, Allen & Unwin, 1977.

Kingsland, K., 'Hatha Yoga Pradipika', London, Grael Communications, 1977.

Krishna, G., 'Kundalini', Shambhala, 1977.

Krishna, G., 'The Secret of Yoga', London, Turnstone Press, 1981.

Lauf, D.I., 'Secret Doctrines of the Tibetan Books of the Dead', Shambhala, 1977.

Luk, C., 'Taoist Yoga', London, Rider, 1970.

Lysbeth, A. Van., 'Pranayama', London, Allen & Unwin, 1979.

Mascaro, J., 'The Upansihads', London, Penguin Books, 1970.

Mascaro, J., 'The Bhagavad Gita', London, Penguin Books, 1970.

Muktananada, S., 'Play of Consciousness', San Francisco, Harper & Row, 1978.

Muktananada, S., 'In The Company of a Siddha', SYDA Foundation, 1978.

Osborne, A., 'Ramana Maharishi – Collected Works', London, Rider, 1969.

Prabavananda, S., 'The Upanishads', New York, Mentor Books, 1957.

Prabavananda, S., 'The Bhagavad Gita', New York, Mentor Books, 1970.

Prabavananda, S., 'Crest Jewels of Discrimination', New York, Mentor Books, 1970.

Prabavananda, S., 'How to Know God', New York, Signet Books, 1969.

Purohit, S., 'Ten Principal Upanishads', London, Faber, 1970.

Radha, S., 'Kundalini Yoga for the West', Shambhala, 1981.

Rajneesh, B.S., 'Roots and Wings', London and Boston, Routledge & Kegan Paul, 1979.

Rajneesh, B.S., 'The Supreme Doctrine', London and Boston, Routledge & Kegan Paul, 1980.

Ramacharaka, 'Fourteen Lessons in Yoga Philosophy', London, Fowler, 1964.

Ramacharaka, 'Science of Breath', London, Fowler, 1964.

Russell, P., 'The T.M. Technique', London, Routledge & Kegan Paul, 1976.

Sannella, Lee, 'Kundalini: Psychosis or Transcendence', San Francisco, Sannella, 1976.

Shah, I., 'Islamic Sufism', New York, Weiser, 1971.

Stephen, D.H., 'Patanjali for Western Readers', London, Theosophical Publishing House, 1957.

Suzuki, D.T., 'Essays in Zen', London, Rider, 1970.

Ushabudha, A., 'Meditation and the Art of Dying', Illinois, Himalayan Institute, 1979.

Vasu, S.C., 'Geranda Samita', London, Theosophical Publishing House, 1976.

Venkatasananda, S., 'The Supreme Yoga (Yoga Vasistha)', London, Chiltern Yoga Trust, 1981.

Wilhelm, R., 'Secret of the Golden Flower', London, Routledge & Kegan Paul, 1962.

Wood, E., 'Yoga', London, Penguin Books, 1970.

Yogananda, P., 'Autobiography of a Yogi', London, Rider, 1975.

Zimmer, H., 'The Philosophies of India', London, Routledge & Kegan Paul, 1951.

INDEX

Vinaya rules, 152
Vira, 105, 109, 110, 114
virya, 97
visasa, 81
vishuddha, 130, 131, 135
Viveka Chudamani, 115–25
Vivekananda, 177
void, 93–4, 97, 98–9, 120
Vyasa, 60, 68, 80

Wentz, W.Y. Evans, 149,
   176
Wilhelm, Richard, 157
Woodroffee, Sir John
   (Arthur Avalon), 106, 176
Wu, Emperor, 155

Yab Yum, 103
Yajur Veda, 121
yama (restraint), 73–4, 164

Yama (God of death), 24,
   143
yana, 91
yantra, 106–7, 112
yatis, 12, 15
Yoga: eight limbs of, 51,
   73–4, 180; sutras, 4,
   69–78; tantra, 111
Yogacara, 98–9, 104, 139,
   153, 158, 161
Yogacarayabhumi, 98
Yogananda, 46, 179–80
Yogeshwari, 177
yoni, 108, 131

zazen, 160
Zen, 7, 148, 153–61
zendos, 158
Zoroastrianism, 173